"What Life I

MW00944792

The Making of a Leader

A Republication of the Autobiography of Dr. Siaka Probyn Stevens

Part II

By Francis Stevens George

ISBN **978-1500923525**

About this work

Twenty-nine years ago, in 1985, one year before he retired from office, Dr. Siaka Probyn Stevens published his Autobiography- 'What Life Has Taught Me'. What Life Has Taught Me is in part a political history of Sierra Leone and in part the story of a self-made man.

This is Part II of the republication of "What Life Has Taught Me". In Part II we visit his childhood, upbringing and education. This work ends with the chapter, "A Study Period at Oxford and London". We have added the Epilogue, which is also found in Part I. The original texts have been reproduced entirely without any changes. We have added extensive footnotes and endnotes where appropriate. We have also added private and official pictures of Dr. Siaka P. Stevens.

The rest of the republication is reproduced in Part I-"The Political Career of Dr. Siaka P. Stevens and Nation-Building".

Siaka Probyn Stevens was the third Prime Minister of Sierra Leone from 1967 to 1971 and the first Executive President of Sierra Leone from 1971 to 1986. Siaka Stevens died on May 29 1988. May His Soul continue to rest in peace.

Dr. Siaka Probyn Stevens continues to influence the politics of Sierra Leone and the lives of Sierra Leoneans. He is part of the history of Sierra Leone. It is therefore important that Sierra Leoneans have access to his autobiography.

This work is published with the expressed permission of The Stevens Family and the Executor of the estate of the Late Dr. Siaka Probyn Stevens.

We acknowledge all those that have contributed to making this project possible. In particular, Ambassadors Jongopie Siaka Stevens and Bockari Kortu Stevens, Mrs. Nemahun Stevens-White for their input into the decisions and outcome of the project.

Last, but by no means least, Dr. Jengo Stevens, Executor of the Estate of the Late Dr. Siaka Probyn Stevens.

Francis Stevens George

August 24th 2014

Table of Contents

Dr. Siaka P. Stevens

I was born into the mud-and-straw world of the masses of the ordinary people of my country. My first patriotism was felt for the small rural community in which my values were moulded and my character formed. All my experience as a politician and a President have taken me back to those peasant ways — and African ways — of making society work by harnessing human compassion, making virtues of necessities and adhering to the great principle of mutu help.

Introduction

The name Siaka P. Stevens is firmly embedded in the political history of Sierra Leone. Dr. Siaka P. Stevens was a pioneer in many ways; (in 1964) he was both leader of the Opposition and Mayor of Freetown simultaneously, a feat yet *unparalleled* and unprecedented in the political history of Sierra Leone; the first Opposition Leader in Africa to lead his Party to Government through the ballot box; the second African President (after Late Julius Nyrere) ever to relinquish power voluntarily; first voices in what became a chorus of protests in Africa over the lending policies of the International Monetary Fund. Subsequent global condemnation of this policy validates Dr. Stevens stand and re-echoes his vision.

What can we therefore learn from his childhood and family life that would give us insights and lessons for upcoming leaders? The republication of this second part of his autobiography is done with this in mind.

To understand and appreciate the politics of Dr. Stevens one needs to know about the childhood and his upbringing. For we cannot truly appreciate some of the decisions of Dr. Stevens until we revisit his childhood. For example, my grandfather's strong opposition to the IMF conditionalities [i] cannot be understood without realizing that for Dr. Stevens, common sense surpassed any academic argument. As Dr. Stevens puts it:

> *My first patriotism was felt for the small rural community in which my values were moulded and my character formed. All my experience as a politician and a President have taken me back to those peasant ways —*

*and African ways — of making society work by
harnessing human compassion, making virtues of
necessities and adhering to the great principle of mutu
help. My childhood home and village life are models of
the basic goodness, which I have striven all my life to
help Sierra Leone and Africa to re-capture on a larger
scale.*

For young Sierra Leoneans, future leaders these chapters hold important lessons. I will cite several. Firstly, your first lesson in leadership starts with your parents, both or one of them. Both of my grandfather parents had a tremendous influence of what he learns about leadership. Integrity, fairness, empathy, hard work, consensus and authority are key ingredients to becoming a good person and a leader.

Secondly, we can learn that knowing yourself and knowing about your world is important. In his book "On Becoming A Leader", Warren Bennis states:

*"By the time we reach puberty, the world has reached us
and shaped us to a greater extent than we realize. Our
family, friends, school, and society in general have told
us-by word and example-how to be. But people begin to
become leaders at that moment when they decide for
themselves how to be".*

In the case of Dr. Stevens, we see this happening very early in his life. Self-knowledge, self-invention were processes that started early with him. In these chapters, we see these qualities manifesting in Dr. Stevens from a very early age.

Dr. Stevens from an early age learned how to take responsibility- responsibility for his community, his duties and most of all his actions. In these pages, we see examples of Siaka P. Stevens demonstrating this- accepting responsibility and blaming no one. Moreover, this trait stayed with him throughout his life.

The third lesson we can take is that community transcends tribal, gender and religious divide. Community means all the people of Sierra Leone. A leader must strive to have the interests of all Sierra Leoneans. Indeed Siaka Stevens own background was a recipe for inclusion of all Sierra Leoneans. As he puts it

I have often said that I am a true representative of my country: my father came from the far north and my mother from the South East. I was born in the centre, at Moyambaii, and spent much of my childhood there among the Mende people.

Later, I was educated in Freetown and worked among the Creoles there. I represented the Freetown West constituency in Parliament, and I married a girl of

---

[1] Rebecca Gustaviana Stevens was born on the 26th October, 1908 in Mange Bureh, Bureh Kasse Makonte Chiefdom. She attended the Harford School for Girls in Moyamba, where she taught and was to later become Matron at the Boarding Home. Her father Francis Alphonso Deveneaux, the first Sierra Leonean District Commissioner was very pleased with his daughter's wedding to Siaka Probyn Stevens, the eldest son of the Limba Tribal Headman in Moyamba and a Christian.

*Temne-Susu origin from the North West. I am proud to
have such a mixed background.*

*I think it has helped me in understanding my
countrymen. Divisiveness has been one of the key
problems in Sierra Leone; too many people have let*

After marriage she left her teaching career to be with her husband in
Lunsar where he worked for the then Delco. After the birth of their
first child and on the death of her father-in-law in 1941 she moved to
Moyamba where she was visited monthly by her husband who
because of his job as a Mineworkers' Union Secretary had to visit
Yengema and Hangha regularly. During her stay in the provinces she
had five more children for her husband before she moved to Freetown
to join her husband, who was then serving as a Protectorate Assembly
man in the Legislative Council in 1951. Her husband was the first
indigenous Minister of Lands, Mines and Labour and it was in
Freetown that she had her last child.

She lost her father in 1955 and in 1957 her husband began his long
stay in political wilderness. With her comforting words and
steadfastness, her husband withstood the storm. Then in 1968 her
loyalty and dedication paid dividends when her husband was sworn-in
as Prime Minister .

With her Christian upbringing, she never stopped praying to the Lord
for the protection of her husband and children. With her children, they
witnessed the swearing-in of her husband as the first Executive
President of the Republic of Sierra Leone in 1971. With her children,
they buried her husband on Sunday, the 12th June, 1988 and at 15.50
hours on Tuesday, 9th October 1990 she passed away. May Her Soul
Continue to Rest in Perfect Peace.

tribal, ethnic or religious loyalties come between them
and their neighbors.

What more can we take from these chapters? For as we know, Stevens was not born into a "ruling "family or privilege. He was a self-made man, who largely educated himself and rose to lead his people. Stevens describe his childhood with pride, something we should note. Stevens does not attempt to paint himself in a different light. He describes with pride his modest upbringing, unpretentiousness and appreciation for the simple things of life.

Sierra Leone has changed significantly since Siaka Stevens wrote his autobiography. Traditional values have been challenged by globalization. Technology has penetrated our cities, towns and even villages.

Yet these chapters offer us insights into the values that we ought to embrace. My grandfather emphasized throughout the chapters the need for a community spirit[iii] and approach to living together and solving our problems.

Dr. Stevens discusses in detail elitism and alerts us to the dangers posed by "people who feel they have a right" to govern. We get an insight into the *damaging* effects of colonialism.

Through his story we see a man who earned everything the hard way; emphasizing hard work, discipline and respect for authority, though not blindly. We see a man who taught others, who believe that knowledge showed be shared for the greater good of one's community and ultimately the nation.

Stevens' talks about the need for citizens through civil society to become part of the Governance of Sierra Leone. As he put it:

> The total good that can flow to a people can never be provided by a government. Ideas for social and economic improvement are not engendered solely by official departments, as those of us who are familiar with the West very well know. In Britain, for instance, not only do non-governmental organizations inspire legislative and other reforms; they also concern themselves with their proper implementation if they are enacted by Parliament.

We see a man who believed common sense; that a leader should distinguish between the problem and the symptoms, and that we should avoid quick fixes.

Though he wrote his story 29 years, many of the values and views he held and expressed are still relevant to our country.

To quote Fred M. Hayward[iv];

> This is also the story of a quite remarkable self-made man. Like many other rural Africans, he received his primary and secondary education away from home through the sacrifices of his family and friends and with the aid of a Creole family in Freetown. Although his formal education stopped, we also after graduation from the Albert Academy (except for a very important stay Africa- Stay at Ruskin College, Oxford in 1947) his education did not. Stevens read in the 1930s widely, taught himself to type while working at the mines,

learned the techniques of broadcasting by memorizing BBC broadcasts, and most importantly learned to read, understand, and lead people. As one can see in this work, the education of Siaka Stevens continues in his late 70s.

One of the refreshing aspects of this autobiography is that Siaka Stevens does not paint himself as an heroic figure. While delighted about his success and proud of his achievements, he also talks about mistakes, errors in judgment, and weaknesses. His comments on the colonial period and nationalist responses demonstrate an openness that clarifies and instructs.

Dr. Stevens, died on May 29th 1988 surrounding by his wife and children in the certain knowledge that he has served his people, and has had a good and enriching life.

William James wrote, in "The Principles of Psychology",

A man's self us the sum total of all that he can call his, not only his body and his psychic powers, but his clothes and his house, his wife and children[v], his ancestors and fiends, his reputation and works, his lands and horses, and yacht and bank account. All these things give him the same emotions. If they wax and prosper, he feels triumphant; if they dwindle and die away, he feels cast down.

Chapter 1
My Home

Recently I came home to Freetown alter a busy visit in Europe. There had been too many meetings, too many people to see, too much sitting in the limited confines of an airplane. I was exhausted but happy because much had been achieved. I went to bed early that night, every limb aching with fatigue.

As I lay there waiting for sleep to come, it was almost as if seventy years had dissolved before my eyes: I was a small boy again, lying on my straw mattress, my feet sore and my back weary. And again I was satisfied that my day had been a full one — a day of helping my father with errands, a day of companionship with my family and neighbors, a day of learning.

Over the years the setting has changed. I more often travel by car or plane than walk barefoot as I did as a child. I no longer feel the hunger, or sense the relish, for food I remember from my boyhood. Moreover, although I still often meet the people from the villages, many of my acquaintances are world statesmen.

Yet through this transformation, I have brought with me the values of the village; and indeed, village life seems never far away from me. The standards of sincerity, hard-work and friendship that I learnt when young have proved to be true and lasting. I am grateful to my parents for the childhood they gave me. Unlike many statesmen, I had no birth right to guarantee me an important place in society.

I was born into the mud-and-straw world of the masses of the ordinary people of my country. My first patriotism was felt for the small rural community in which my values were molded and my character formed. All my experience as a politician and a President have taken me back to those peasant ways — and African ways — of making society work by harnessing human compassion, making virtues of necessities and adhering to the great principle of mutu help. My childhood home and village life are models of the basic goodness, which I have striven all my life to help Sierra Leone and Africa to re-capture on a larger scale.

This is the theme of my story. By turning to our African experience with reverence and love, we can find the sources for the kind of society we want to build today in Africa and bequeath to the future. The peasant communities of my childhood had no material advantages. They were contented because they knew no other way of real life, and hardworking because their very survival depended on the amount and quality of the food they could produce.

The village was like one large family, each household pooling its labor resources to work one another's farms in turn. The men planted and harvested the rice; the women weeded and watered it. While there was precious little money most of the year, nobody lacked the necessities of life; nobody in trouble was without help and sympathy, and in times of bad harvest, what little food there was shared equally among the families.

Hoarding, stealing, uncooperative or anti-social behavior were rare. Disputes there were, of course, human being what it

14

is, but if these could not be settled amicably among the parties concerned, there was always the Chief to resort to, with the overall guidance the community gave through custom and the sheer necessity of mutual dependence.

My earliest memories are of little things — the sights, smells, and tastes of childhood spent exploring elementary experience with a wonder I can still vividly recall. I remember my family at prayers. I remember the awesome steam trains, their disciplined pounding and wild screams and the smell of hot metal and steam in my nostrils. I remember our neighbors' smiles. I remember meals and the warming taste of our savory rice and the feel of it in my belly, all my taste buds and gastric senses alert with boyish hunger. Most of all I remember the love of my family and the wisdom and goodness of my father.

By worldly standards, my father was a modest, simple man, but he filled the little world of our household and his orders and example dominated our lives. He was illiterate; but, thanks to the efforts and sacrifices he made, I became the first of his line to get a formal education. His goodness and uprightness gave him a wisdom — a kind of insight and human understanding which most educated people lack. He had what you might call a popular learning, a learning he had picked up by observing and listening and reaping the lore and traditions of rural life. Piety and unstinting toil earned him a place of respect in society and work and thrift gradually brought him the basis of a modest sufficiency as a result I was able to go to school and get a good start in life. He seemed to inherit all the best virtues of his tribe, the Limbas.

The Limba tribe[vi] is one of the most important in Sierra Leone and is divided into a number of sub-tribes, such as the Tonko-Limbas, Brewa Limbas and Saffroko Limbas. The people have earned themselves a reputation for palm wine tapping, honesty and fidelity. They are very rarely involved in court cases, and are in great demand in positions of trust.

The Limbas were not a self-seeking or deliberately ambitious people, and few of them sought contact with the Europeans and Creoles on the coast. Other tribes regarded them as backward and somewhat simple-minded. They remained cut off from the southern tribes for a long time, for there was little in Limba country to attract outsiders; the land was not particularly fertile, there were no large-scale mining operations, no industries, no railway connections and poor road links. Those that did not migrate to Freetown and other towns tended to live together under their own headmen, retain their tribal dress and customs and seemed slower than most tribes to integrate with city life.

Because of the stigma attached to them, many Limbas who came from the north-west of the territory bordering on Temne land passed themselves off as Temnes in the belief that this would add to their prestige. I was amused early in my Presidency when I was told that a certain countryman of mine who had long posed as a Temne went to the headmaster of the school where his son was a pupil and asked that the records be changed to show his son as a Limba. "After all," he said, "things are different now that we have a Limba as President."

The Gallinas tribe to which my mother belonged, inhabit the extreme south-east of Sierra Leone near the border with Liberia where many of them live and they pass from one country to the other regardless of the boundary.

On my mother's side, I was related to King Siaka of Geindayma (Gendama) who was a powerful man in Gallinas country in the 1890s. He even corresponded with Queen Victoria. Gendama today still bears traces of its historic importance — the old road (a rare thing in the Protectorate in the old days), the ancient cannon guarding the line of the creek which leads up from the Atlantic, and the reminders of the slave trade that once brought an obnoxious prosperity to the little town.

When I paid a visit to Gendama in 1974 the old people performed some of their atavistic ceremonies in honour of the dead. In the middle of these echoes of the past I landed by helicopter— a nice juxtaposition of tradition and technology which is typical of modern Sierra Leone. I warmed to the old-timer who told me on my walk-about, "I wish- King Siaka could get up from his grave and see what is happening in Gendama today!"

Perhaps the most outstanding thing about the Gallinas is the fact that it is the only tribe in this part of Africa which developed a writing of its own, the Vai Alphabet[vii]. It is said that it originated when an elder of the tribe observed that a European trader made some marks on a piece of paper as a commercial transaction was being negotiated and later referred to his notes to recall facts and figures with great accuracy. The elder then decided to devise his own system of recording relevant facts — a system which was eventually developed by members of the tribe into a full alphabet.

One would have expected such an improvised system of writing to be ideographic, as most of the early systems were, with various signs standing for objects, concepts or figures. The remarkable thing about the Vai alphabet is that the elder who conceived it hit straight away on the idea of a phonetical system with signs standing for various sounds used in the tribal dialect. If I ever get some time for leisure in my life, I would like to do some research on the old Via culture.

> *I have often said that I am a true representative of my country: my father came from the far north and my mother from the south east. I was born in the centre, at Moyamba, and spent much of my childhood there among the Mende people. Later, I was educated in Freetown and worked among the Creoles there. I represented the Freetown West constituency in Parliament, and I married a girl of Temne-Susu origin from the North West. I am proud to have such a mixed background.*

I think it has helped me in understanding my countrymen. Divisiveness has been one of the key problems in Sierra Leone; too many people have let tribal, ethnic or religious loyalties come between them and their neighbors.

It has often surprised me that people do not always put their fellow beings first. In the village where I grew up, helping other people was one of the first lessons that every child learnt. My father was a strong upholder of the values of kindliness to others — always, in the case of his children, tempered with firmness!

My father's family, like most people living in the northern region of Sierra Leone, were farmers as had been their forebears for generations past. Their main crop was upland rice, which was grown with great physical hardship on the steep hills north, and east of the territory, some of which rose to heights of 2,000 ft (609m).

On the plains, 400 ft. (123m) above sea level, much of which was swamp, other crops were grown such as groundnuts, millet, cassava, sweet potatoes and maize. But whatever the crop, nothing grew without sheer hard work and the constant attention of the farmers and their families.

My father's neighbors were peace-loving, honest men and women who derived pleasure after a day's hard labour from one another's companionship around a calabash of palm wine, relaxing with their children or playing Warn — a game for two people who use a special board and some pebbles. When we were adolescents, my father enjoyed telling us about the earlier years of his life.

He used to recall that after the evening meal, and when he had finished the various chores expected of him, he would join the group of older men who gathered each evening to chat about the state of the crops, local happenings and the latest news gleaned from people who had returned from places further afield.

He listened to their grouses about the injustice of the Protectorate hut tax and heard how rumor had it that the monies so collected were being used for developing Freetown and the Colony instead of the Protectorate where schools, hospitals, roads, railways and bridges were desperately needed. He heard mention of fascinating jobs that some local boys had landed in Freetown and the complaints that the opportunities there were attracting the cream of Protectorate youth away from the land.

My father was a man who liked to see things for himself and he was interested to see what was going on in the Colony. So, as he had an adventurous spirit and, at that time, little responsibility, he set off on the long trek to Freetown - a distant, terrifying metropolis by the standards of my father's world. But because he had never had the opportunity of an education he found when he got there that the only openings that were available to him were in poorly paid laboring jobs.

He decided that if it were a question of living below the bread line he would rather do that back home, where at least food and lodging would be assured. But just as he was about to leave he caught sight of a recruiting poster for the Royal West African Frontier Force which somebody interpreted for his benefit. It seemed the very job for him. He presented himself at the headquarters and was immediately accepted.

The Sierra Leone Battalion, which was formerly known as the Police Frontier Force, numbered in those days 629 men, 550 of whom were privates. Its officers and men had recently been highly commended for the part they played in the Ashanti War in the Gold Coast in 1900 when, as scouts for the advancing column that went to the relief of Kumasi, they discovered the enemy and fought with such courage that one of their number, Private Amadu, was promoted sergeant on the spot and was later awarded the Distinguished Service Order[viii].

In those days, of course, it was common practice for the colonial powers to use troops from one Colony to conquer another, or to put down a rebellion. Unfortunately, Africans innocently lent themselves to this practice as the spirit of African unity and solidarity had not yet swept the Continent.

As a raw recruit, my father was paid 6d. a day which was raised to 9d. upon his appointment being confirmed. He was also issued with trousers and boots. This may seem so normal a procedure for an army recruit that people may wonder at my bothering to mention it.

Nevertheless, in fact had my father joined up a few years later, in 1909, he would have been ordered to walk barefoot and wear khaki shorts. Nobody could give a reason for this extraordinary action on the part of the authorities, but our army boys marched bootless for thirty years or more until "agitators" like the late I. T. A. Wallace-Johnson[ix] brought pressure to bear and got the issue of boots re-introduced.

I remember my father telling me of the time he was sent to Liberia. The soldiers were not paid on time, so one day they raised such hell that the Liberian government had to ask Freetown to recall them! When he was back in Freetown he took his turn mounting guard at Government House, the official residence of the British Colonial Governor. I often wonder what he would have said had he known that one day his own son would become the lawful occupier of Government House.

I know he would have been very happy and perhaps a little surprised that a guard's son should become President. Whenever I think of him standing on guard outside the very building in which I now labour as Chief Executive of my country, I feel a surge of pride in my roots and a renewed sense of oneness with my people.

Sir Leslie Probyn[2], who was Governor at that time, must have made a very favorable impression on my father, for when I was born he named me Siaka Probyn. My name of Probyn was not the only reminder of Dad's army career, for our family name was permanently changed because of this period of his life.

He enlisted as James Tibin and was discharged as James Stevens. It seemed that when the European officers yelled 'Tibin!' it sounded like 'Steven', so much so that many people thought his name actually was Steven or Stevens, and as he raised no objection, it stuck and he continued to use it from then on.

Before long my father was posted to Moyamba, about 75 miles from Freetown, as part of a military expedition launched by

---

[2] Sir **Leslie Probyn** (1862-1938) KCMG was an administrator for the British Empire

the British Administration. There he became orderly to a sergeant major called Norman, whose granddaughter, Miatah Massaquoi, was staying with him. My father married her and later she became my mother.

From Moyamba my father was posted to Gbonjeima which was at that time a stronghold of the Mende tribal warriors. The Mendes were, and are, one of the largest tribes in Sierra Leone. They were more fortunate than other tribes in the hinterland in that when Western education eventually began to penetrate inland from the Creole- populated strip of coastland known as the Colony, schools were established in their territory some little time before they were in the more northerly parts of the country.

As a result, the Mendes[x] became the first of all other tribes in Sierra Leone to be able to challenge the Creoles[xi] for the so-called 'white collar' jobs which had previously been the sole preserve of the educated Creoles.

Soon after my brother Kortu was born, the period for which my father had signed on for military service expired. Instead of re-enlisting for another nine years he asked to be discharged. Undoubtedly, the increasing responsibilities of marriage coupled with fatherhood had had a settling effect on him and made him anxious to establish roots, to be his own boss and master in his own house. Maybe, too, his boots were wearing out and he had heard the rumor that he would shortly be expected to march barefoot!

With his gratuity from the army of £20 he bought a supply of liquor, tobacco and provisions and set up a small shop in Gbonjeima. Whenever the stock needed replenishing my mother had to travel a distance often miles each way to Sembehun on the Bagru River to buy what was necessary from the large commercial firms there. It is really only in retrospect that I am able to appreciate fully how tough was the fight for survival in those days.

At the time it seemed no hardship that our women should trudge miles on end down dusty tracks under the scorching sun, weighted down either by pregnancy or a baby strapped to the back, or both, plus an enormous head-load of items they hoped to trade for a few miserable pennies profit. It was all a part of the everyday scene, all we had ever known.

There was no easy way to keep body and soul together. My father took two other wives, Mabondo and Memuna, both of whom belonged to leading families in Gbonjeima. This was a great help to my mother who now had others with whom she could share her workload. My mother was a devout Muslim and my father was a Christian.

He had chosen Christianity because he sincerely believed in its doctrine, even though it is not a religion ideally suited to the traditional African way of life. It had gained the title of the 'white man's religion', and, like all European ideas and ways of doing things, it was un-African and quite alien to us.

Because of these difficulties many Africans, although attracted by the fundamental precepts of the Christian church, have been unwilling to participate because it would go against their traditional life style. One of the stumbling blocks for any African considering Christianity is that of monogamy versus polygamy. This was certainly a problem for my father, for although he was a devout Christian, he saw nothing wrong with polygamy.

The fact that he officiated in church as a sides man made his practice of polygamy doubly hard for the clergy to suffer, but no matter how often the pastor admonished him for the number of wives he had, it had no effect whatsoever. I well remember the day when the pastor brought to our two-storey mud-brick house the bishop of the Mission, an American who was visiting Sierra Leone.

Together they tackled my father on the subject of polygamy and a fierce argument ensued in an upstairs room. Then my father called to me to bring up my mothers. There were five of them and they stood dutifully in line before him. "Now this one," he said, indicating my real mother, "is Siaka's mother.

This one, as you can see, is suckling her newly born child. This one next to her is about to give birth to her second child. This one has year-old twins and this one was put in my care by my dying father. Now I would like you to choose from among them the one I ought to keep and those I must drive away."

The two church dignitaries shook their heads in bewilderment and were forced to concede defeat. "As I have said many times before," my father said,

> **"You may take Siaka and Kortu and do with them what you like, but please leave me in peace to live with my wives."**

The human usefulness of polygamy for my father's household and for the society in which it was embedded shows how the African has always evolved the social conventions best suited to his environment, without interference from outside. The attitude of the church authorities' shows how alien dogmas, insensitively applied, however well intentioned, are a negative — even destructive — influence on Africa.

If polygamy dies out — and already many husbands find the economic advantages of monogamy irresistible — it will be because of changes in the total social and economic context and, in particular, because of the changing role and aspirations of women. It will not be because of the strength of European ethical conventions, or because there is anything morally wrong with polygamy. I have always been amused at outsiders' attitudes to this highly organized African custom.

The parting words from a kindly Cockney[xii] butcher to me when I left London in 1948 were, So yer'll be returnin' 'ome to yer nine wives, lad". I could do nothing but reply with a wink (while I laughed inwardly at the note of envy in his voice),

"How right you are! But what can a man do? You see, we have no brothels in Africa!"

Polygamous marriages are entered into in such a serious manner that the rights of each wife, from the most senior to the most junior are highly protected. Far from each wife being jealous of the others, they are usually very companionable together, sharing household duties and becoming firm friends. Indeed often a wife may be selected by the senior wife who, in any case, must always be consulted before a marriage takes place.

Each woman knows her place and what is expected of her. It is the senior wife alone who receives orders from her husband to be passed on to the other women, and it is she who decides which of them shall share the man's bed each night. It is the duty of the wife whose turn it is to sleep with the husband to cook his food that day and prepare his room.

To my mind the African has far more wisdom and honesty than the European in his attitude towards relationships between men and women, for it is often unrealistic to advocate one woman for one man. Harmony and happiness in a monogamist's household often depend very much on the man's success at secrecy coupled with the wife's willingness to turn a blind eye.

One might say that in every monogamist there is the natural polygamist struggling to get out, and the fact that in non-African countries brothels abound, divorce courts are overworked and paternity orders are hotly contested suggests that monogamy is not so blissful as its supporters would have us believe.

The African Christian gets round the difficult question of monogamy demanded by the Christian Church by marrying one wife according to the rites of the Church and other wives according to native customs. Coming from a home both Christian and Muslim I feel I have gained an insight into each of these religions and, although I am nothing more than a layman on religious topics, I do have very decided views. It has always seemed to me that Islam has much to commend it as religion for the African.

The few demands it makes on him are straightforward and only concerned with practical religion. It does not interfere with his customs and traditional way of life. In the case of Christianity, however, worship does not seem to be so simple. The differences between sects of the Christian Church may be impossible to bridge, whereas although there are as many as 72 sects in the Muslim faith, members of any sect can worship quite happily in the same mosque.

But a Roman Catholic may be unwilling to attend a Methodist service and an Anglican would feel unfamiliar with a Greek Orthodox service. Christians seem, then, separated rather than united, even when they belong to the same country and race as Catholics and Protestants do in Northern Ireland.

I believe that the simpler the demands made on man by any religion the more likelihood there is of him leading a saintlier life. This is not to decry the virtues of love, charity, tolerance and humility, but rather to emphasize that so long as a man lives decently and properly there should be no question of his private affairs being interfered with by any authoritative body, religious or otherwise. And I know that in his own way my father fulfilled his obligations.

He loved and cared for all his wives and children; he was a good father and good husband and a valuable member of the community. He sought God with a sincere heart in depth of faith, which is the essence of all true religion. And yet all the pastor could do was complain that my father was a polygamist! My father's army training had made him into a disciplinarian.

Sometimes my brother and I were a little afraid of him, although we always respected him. As soon as we were able to walk we had to join the men folk and lend a hand with the cultivation of crops, the care of animals, the building of shelters — in short, the art of survival. We were all expected to pull our weight, whatever our age. But it was not all work and no play.

Kortu and I were mischievous young boys and sometimes we tried to escape from the daily chores so that we could nm off into the woods and hunt small animals, climb trees, play rowdy games or search for fruit and berries to eat. But when we returned home punishment awaited us in the form of a good spanking and extra tasks to perform.

Some of the pranks we got up to caused my parents much anxiety, for we were highly adventurous and scared of nothing. One day my father bought a bull which be believed was securely tethered in the compound. Kortu, who was very young at the time, wandered outside on his own and became interested in this fierce looking beast, going up close and no doubt teasing it.

Suddenly a piercing yell from Kortu brought everybody rushing out of the house in alarm. The bull had broken loose, charged at his tormentor and made a deep ugly gash on his forehead. It was lucky for Kortu that he lived to tell the tale and was left with no more than a scar as a permanent reminder of his foolhardiness.

My father, who had never received a formal education, was very anxious that his own children should be educated. In fact, he had managed to pick up a little bit of reading and counting in the army, but not enough to satisfy him. I remember how he used to struggle with reading his Bible on Sunday afternoons. Because of this he was more determined than ever that his children should have the benefit of education. He was also greatly egged on by a neighbor of ours, Margaret Barber, affectionately known as Mammy Barber, who always said "Sergeant Stevens, sen dem pikin go school o!"

He told me once how hard he prayed when in Gbonjeima that he might get something to do in Moyamba so that he could send us to school. His prayer was answered, for in 1911, with the help of his army discharge certificate, he was appointed as contractor to supply food to the central prison in Moyamba.

Although I had been born in Moyamba I could remember nothing about it, for I was only an infant when we left. Now, at the age of 6 or so, I returned to my birth place as a stranger, and a very astonished stranger at that. Gbonjeima, the only place I had ever known, had seemed very big to my childish eyes and the idea that bigger places might exist never entered my head.

Suddenly, as I found myself in this large, busy and important-looking town, Gbonjeima shriveled into insignificance in my mind. Two and even three storied houses lined the streets; there were two schools, a number of big commercial firms, the Circuit Court which was the Supreme Court of the Protectorate, the central prison and the gallows which the colonial administration found to be very necessary in those days.

Within a very short time of our arrival in Moyamba the town was colorful with flags and bunting to celebrate the coronation of King George V of Great Britain and Ireland, the British Dominions beyond the seas, Defender of the Faith, Emperor of India and under whose sovereignty we also were. I had no idea what all the excitement was about but I remember being given a china mug which stunned me at the time because it was the first gift of such splendor I had ever received.

When the message somehow got through to me that this glistening colored object was mine, I clutched it possessively to my chest, afraid that somebody who hadn't got one themselves might take it from me. We sat at long tables in the Market Place and stuffed ourselves with food, much of which I had never tasted before.

I soon became very well acquainted with the central prison because every day of my father's contract I helped carry heavy loads of cassava, greens and other food and deliver them at the prison gates. I shall never forget those daily journeys as long as I live. It is not the memory of the loads I carried nor the distance I had to travel that haunts me, because my home was not that far from the prison, but the torture I suffered from tiny flea-like insects called jiggers which jump about in the dust and settle on human flesh, especially between the toes and on the soles of the feet.

Once they attach themselves to you they never let go, but burrow their way into the flesh and remain there, sucking the blood and growing bigger and bigger until the pain they cause becomes unbearable. It was impossible to avoid these jiggers because the tracks we had to use were infested with them. There were no tarred roads at that time and no heavy lorries to crush the sharp stones, so that trying to negotiate that gritty uneven surface while jiggers burrowed their way painfully into the soles of my feet became a positive nightmare.

A woman in our household who was given the job of removing these pests from my feet made the pain doubly worse by treating the sores with limes.

I always associate jiggers with *akarah*, a sort of cake made from a mixture of banana and rice which is fried in palm oil after having been allowed to ferment for a while. It was delicious and was made by a Mammy Tigidah, who was our next-door neighbor. After these jiggers had sucked blood from my toes all night, I used to wake up in the morning feeling so hungry that the one longing I had was to fill my stomach with *akarah*. I promised myself that when I became an engine driver and got a salary at the end of each month, I would buy lots of Mammy Tigidah's *akarah*.

To be an engine driver was my greatest ambition. On every possible occasion I used to rush to the railway station to watch the daily passenger train arrive. With hero worship in my eyes, I gazed at the engine driver going through his routine: refreshing himself from a bottle, checking a valve, moving a brass lever, touching this gadget and that, waiting for the guard's whistle and then touching his oily cap in a farewell greeting as he brought his steaming, hissing monster to life. To me he was no ordinary man, but somebody very special, the ultimate in manhood. How could a boy aspire to be anything less?

I began my education at the mission school of the Evangelical United Brethren. The present Harford boarding school for girls was then a day school and the girls used to join us in the school building for lessons and return home after school. I remember many of them — Virginia and Beatrice Morgan, Laura Dove, Hawa Jumu, Amanda and Nellie Weaver and Flora Caulker, and several U.B.C. missionaries, such as Eta Odle and Miss Shanklin, who used to invite us to their mission home on Sunday afternoons and give us sweets. Because of my association with the Harford, I am sometimes tempted to describe myself as an old boy of the Harford Girls' School!

It is common practice in Sierra Leone for a man living in the more remote areas to send his children to live with friends in the principal towns so that they can attend the schools there. As soon as my father moved to Moyamba many of his friends took advantage of the situation.

Quite suddenly our household increased by about 15 boys! For Kortu and me it was the greatest fun having so many companions with whom to play and share the work, but I cannot imagine how my parents retained their sanity, especially at mealtimes when pandemonium broke loose.

The food was put into two big bowls each of which was allocated to seven or eight boys. Immediately the bowls appeared on the mud floor they were pounced upon by a ravenous, shouting hoard, each boy shoving and elbowing his way to get nearest to the food, some grabbing portions of rice and stuffing them into whatever container was most handy, others cramming as much as they could into their mouths.

Fortunately for my parents our days were so planned that there was little time for us to fool around and get up to mischief. My military- minded father saw to that. We had to be up at 6 a.m. to take food to the prison. On our return we had a bath and breakfast and then went to school. Our afternoons were taken up buying the prisoners' food for the following day, fetching wood for the fire, running errands and doing any other job that my parents asked us to do. When all these chores were properly completed, we were free to swim in the river and enjoy ourselves.

Our pleasures were simple and we were so thrilled with the little that was offered us. Bits of wood, a rusty wheel rim, old boxes, pebbles, all kinds of junk were converted into playthings and highly prized. I never possessed a toy from a shop. To spend hard-earned money on such trivia when there were stomachs to fill and bodies to clothe would have been unthinkable.

My father established contact with a lot of prominent people all over Sierra Leone during these years because Moyamba was the centre for what was known as the circuit court, which was the highest court in the Protectorate as it then was. Now and again chiefs and other prominent people from as far away as Kabala, Kenema and Kailahun would meet in Moyamba for sessions of the court, as well as prominent lawyers from Freetown, such as Pa Barrett. I used to accompany my father when he visited the Paramount Chief or some other big personality in the evening, and I would sit down in a corner to listen to their conversation.

This is customary, and it gives a child, even at that early age, an insight into what is going on. The District Commissioner was often the subject of conversation at these pow-wows and he seemed to me, in my childish way, to be a bogeyman. The D.C. was held in dread all over the country — so much so that when my father called us to prayers he would readily add "And save us, o Lord, from the trouble of the D.C."! I suppose all children have a figure in their imagination that they hold in fear and dread, but perhaps the District Commissioner was a more unusual choice than the customary witches and goblins that have a place in most people's recollections.

As I look back on my childhood, I am often surprised that it is the small and seemingly unimportant incidents that are most vivid in my mind. In retrospect I can see that often these events were more special than one gave credit for at the time. One such incident I remember in particular. My mother, being of the Islamic faith, dressed Kortu and me in Muslim dress when we first went to school. I liked this type of garment very much because under the flowing gown we wore satin shirts which had two very useful pockets.

As we passed through my father's shop on our way to school we used to pick up biscuits and smuggle them out in these concealed pockets. We thought it was a huge joke to trick my father, who was always so smart and alert. Then one morning he called us back. "Come here a minute," he said, his hands immediately alighting on the tell-tale bulges in our top pockets. "So this is what you get up to when my back is turned, is it?"

My father taught me humility and honesty, disciplined me, but never to excess. His punishments always fitted our crimes, and I admired him for his sense of fairness. His determination to do right for his sons impressed me, so that even now, years later, I can look back on my childhood with warmth and affection, remembering it with happiness -apart, of course, from the jiggers!

Chapter 2
My Schooling

When I was nine years old my father decided that the time had come to send me to Freetown where I would have the chance of a higher standard of education and an opportunity to mix with boys from many different tribes and social backgrounds. For children at school in Sierra Leone today it is hard to imagine what education was like when I was a boy.

The subjects taught in schools then were not geared towards producing good African citizens, knowledgeable about their culture and heritage, but rather merely to produce men who would be capable of holding administrative posts in the colonial regime. Children found themselves learning about British history and politics, while they knew very little about their own country. It was only recently that I learnt the name of one of our major rivers, at a time when the Thames, the Seine and the Tiber were names already familiar to me.

This has struck me as being absurd and I have consistently campaigned for a more African orientated syllabus in our schools. But in my young days it was not only the lessons that left much to be desired; the emphasis was on educating the Colony — the small colonial enclave around Freetown — not the Protectorate, where the vast majority of the people lived; and in the Protectorate those who did receive a formal education were usually of chiefly and other leading families. I need hardly say that this was a very undesirable situation.

On a personal level, however, it makes the determination and doggedness of my father all the more remarkable. I was not the son of a chief and my family was poor, my prospects of an education in the Colony were far from bright if it had not been for the sacrifices my father made I probably would not even have learnt to spell my name! But he had set his heart on sending me to Freetown, and his wish eventually came true.

He spent some time looking for a reliable guardian for me, for Freetown was no place for a young and inexperienced country lad to roam around where he pleased. Fortunately, an old army friend of my father had a son, a train guard called Mr. Smith. He and his wife Okeke lived in Kissy, which was then a little village a few miles outside of Freetown, and they kindly agreed to take me under their wing.

Clutching my few possessions, I set out with my father to board the train from Moyamba to Kissy. It was my first parting from my family, but I was so excited about the prospect of this great adventure and so full of hopes and plans for the future, that any feelings of sadness I might have had were temporarily numbed. And above all, awaiting me was the tremendous thrill of five-and-a-half to six hours journey on a train. The railway was still quite a novelty even for my father, for the whole project was only begun eighteen years previously and was not completed until 1906.

I can remember feeling very glad that my father was to accompany me on the train journey, for although I was thrilled at the thought of independence and a new school in a huge and exciting town, I was also a little anxious. At each stop there were crowds of people standing on the station platforms, greeting newly arrived friends or waving goodbye to departing relatives. There were women traders who tried to sell their wares to the hungry and thirsty passengers.

Most of all I remember the feeling of butterflies in my stomach as we crawled at a snail's pace across a deep ravine. I peered down far below me at the swirling water. I recall with shame how I half prayed for some dreadful catastrophe that would send us hurtling down the ravine. That would have been a real adventure! It seems impossible to me now that a nine year-old boy should be so unaware of death and destruction. And yet one cannot help but admire the simplicity of youth which sees only adventure in even the most desperate situations.

It seemed as if all too soon we arrived at Waterloo Station, which was only about twenty-five miles away from Freetown. We were told that the train would wait there for some considerable time. "In that case," my father said to our carriage companions, with whom he had made friends, "we might as well get out and stretch our legs." As he intended to combine this exercise with a drink of palm wine, he told me to wait patiently where I was until he returned. After a while I felt the carriage give a jolt, then to my horror the train started to move off. I leant out of the window, shouted and gesticulated, but there was no sign of my father and

I could not stop the train. It was late when the train pulled into Kissy station and it was a somewhat anxious and subdued youngster who clambered down from the carriage and with a very crushed bundle tucked under one arm, stood timidly and apprehensively on the platform to take stock of the lonely situation in which he found himself. "Are you lost, boy?" a kindly official asked me. I explained to him what had happened and he took care of me until my father arrived some hours later to claim me and take me to my new home.

Before he left me to return to Moyamba, he impressed upon me my good fortune in being able to attend school in the capital, in having Mr. and Mrs. Smith to care for me and in the great future that lay within my grasp if I made the utmost of every opportunity that would come my way.

"Remember, son," he said, "whatever you do here will reflect on us at home and I know you won't discredit us by shirking your duties either in school or in the house. Do whatever you are asked to do willingly and to the best of your ability. If you get into a mess that is not of your own making I will always stand by you, but I'll never lend a hand to a sloven or a sloth."

He stressed that whilst it was important to be proud of my own tribe, my home and my parents, I must respect the fact that strangers I would meet would feel equally proud of theirs, that I must never let these feelings turn to arrogance or allow them to come between me and my friends, that I must learn to be tolerant and understanding of other people's customs and ideas.

As I take stock of what now seems to be an increasingly intolerant world, I cannot but be grateful for my father's advice. It was good advice and I have always tried to practice it. If only more people could have heard Dad's words of wisdom!

I tried to be as helpful as possible in the Smith household. My day began at 5 a.m. when I would light the fire and sweep the compound. Once the fire was hot enough I would warm up the stew or palaver sauce which had been prepared the previous evening, and on Mondays, Wednesdays and Fridays I would pack some of this with rice in a 'chop box' which I carried to Kissy railway station for Mr. Smith to take with him on his train journey up country. On my return to the house at about 7 a. m. it was time to escort Mrs. Smith to Freetown to help carry the large bundles of merchandise which she traded there.

As soon as I off-loaded these, I rushed back to Kissy as fast as my legs would carry me to bath and prepare myself for school which was the Wesleyan Primary School in Kissy. Even when school finished at 3 p.m. there was no time for me to hang around, chat and play games with my schoolmates for my schedule was so tight that it simply did not allow for it. Instead I had to rush back home, cook a pot of rice for the evening meal, sweep the yard again to rid it of mango leaves and other rubbish that had collected during the day, and then leave for Freetown once more to collect Mrs. Smith and her wares which now included a supply of fresh fish or meat and other provisions that she had bought for our supper.

On Tuesdays, Thursdays and Saturdays my next duty was to meet Mr. Smith at the railway station and carry back his empty food container. After I had eaten my meal and washed the dishes it was time for bed, and I was certainly ready for it!

Alternatively, sometimes after school I would go out selling kerosene by the bottle and we had a special way of shouting 'Ker-ro sene-ya' at the top of our voices. We liked hawking kerosene: we young rascals could get together and swap news. Heaven only knows what we discussed in those days but we were always chattering away.

It was only now that I learnt to talk Krio. Coming from up-country I did not know much Krio and the boys used to laugh at me, but soon I was luxuriating in phrases like, *'You sabbi but you nor know!' or'Gi am fedder!'* To me it was a delightful language, full of the opulent creativity and imagination of the Creole people. It had a bit of French, a bit of Portuguese, a bit of Yoruba in it. It was as rich as a patchwork of diverse bits of the history of Sierra Leone.

Saturday was always a particularly busy day, because it was laundry day. In addition to my normal chores I had to help with the washing. Mrs. Smith did not go to Freetown on Saturdays and spent most of her time preparing food for the following day. I can still remember the taste of that food: groundnut stew, pepper soup, the famous Creole palaver sauce, peppery beef, tripe, bologie leaves, palm oil and dried 'bonga'. There was also foo-foo, which we helped to make by pounding softened cassava with a pestle and mortar. It was a boring job, but my efforts were always rewarded when I sat down to eat the delicious food.

I did not resent my heavy work load, for I was grateful for the kindness the Smiths had shown me by taking me in, but one thing that did annoy me was the attitude of many Creole families towards children from the Protectorate who were put into their care. My position in the household was that of a servant. I was even something of a slave to the children! With me around to fetch and carry, sweep and clean, they were free to play, study or do whatever they liked. At my home in Moyamba everybody in the house was expected to pull their weight until too old or infirm to do so. Sometimes during those days in Kissy I had firmly to repeat to myself my father's advice always to be willing and helpful.

Often it was these words alone that helped me to check my tears, for I felt like crying at what seemed to me such injustice. Although at the time I would never have guessed that one day I would be grateful for this training, I now see that this self-discipline was an invaluable lesson. I often think that if it had not been for this I would still be somewhere at the bottom of the ladder. Moreover, because my playtime was so limited it became all the more precious to me, and I learnt to use it well, not wasting one minute of it. My days in Kissy taught me the basis of successful living: how to work hard and how to play hard, and, most important of all, how to keep the two separate.

Kissy in those days was cut off from Freetown by thick bush and during the day people went there to gather firewood, search for fruit and trap small animals for the stewpot. Gradually over the years more and more of the bush was cleared to make way for buildings and roads until the village of Kissy and the city of Freetown became so linked that it was difficult to tell where one ended and the other began. A house that marked the boundary between the two places was owned at one time by an ex-telegraph inspector I knew, called Mr. Leigh.

When I first visited Freetown I thought it was a terrifying

place and whenever I accompanied Mrs. Smith with her loads during my first few weeks there I kept close behind her for fear of getting lost among the pushing, jostling crowds of people. There were so many streets to confuse me, such high buildings hemming me in, hazards to watch for, like bicycles and hammocks barging their way through the congested thoroughfare, with traders noisily touting their wares and hosts of beggars squatting hopefully outside the large stores. One worry was spared me at least, for there were no cars in those days to add to my confusion.

On my first visit to Freetown, I returned home to my 'Missus' — as I called Mrs. Smith — with cuts all over my feet. I was so busy looking up awestruck at the tops of buildings, the like of which I had never seen before — instead of watching the road — that I stepped on some sharp pieces of broken glass. The tallest building I had ever seen was a Syrian trader's house in Moyamba, with sleeping quarters above the shop. I had never imagined the rest of the world could be so different.

I found it very difficult to get used to the number of rogues that abounded in Freetown. At home in Moyamba most people did what they could to help one another and few would think of taking something that was not theirs by right. In spite of Mrs. Smith's frequent warnings to me to be on my guard, I still found it hard to mistrust people.

A few months after I had arrived in the capital, Mrs. Smith sent me to buy a glass for a kerosene lamp from a French store called Perineaux, near the Sawpit Wharf steps. As I was standing in the street, gazing in bewilderment into the store and wondering if it was the right place, a man came up to me. He was wearing the usual thread bare trouser and an old black jacket. "Can I help you?" he asked me kindly, no doubt aware that I was a stranger in town.

I told him what I wanted and showed him the money I had in my hand. "Give me the money and wait here a minute," he said, "I'll go in and get it for you." I was impressed by his friendliness and gladly handed over the cash, for being somewhat shy by nature, big stores overwhelmed me as they still do. As the time went by and he did not appear I began to be anxious and timidly peered into the shop to see if I could see him.

There was no sign of him and the store was preparing to shut down for the night. My heart sank into my stomach and tears of anger and disappointment welled up in my eyes. Now my problem was: how to return home? I could not dare tell my Missus I'd been gulled. I was hiding in the compound in the dark and before long Mrs. Smith spied me and asked what had happened. I told her that I had met a man at the shop and had given the money to him. I prefer not to recall the language that she used, but I think I remember one sentence: "Dis kossoh dog!" She then gave me a good hiding.

It was a hard lesson to learn, and, to a small trusting boy, it was impossible to imagine that such dishonesty abounded. My training up country in farm work, in hunting and trapping animals and in keeping a weather eye open for dangers in the bush had developed my powers of observation and senses of sight to a high degree. On the Saturday morning following my encounter with the thief I was sent to the Big Wharf to buy firewood.

My senses were suddenly alerted by a suspicious movement somewhere in the crowd. As I fixed my eyes in its direction I spotted a man trying to slink unobtrusively into the background out of sight. At once I recognized him as the man who had tricked me over the lamp glass. I hung on to him like a baby monkey clinging to its mother, meanwhile shouting at the top of my voice: *"Tifi Tifi"* Soon a crowd surrounded us and a policeman came along. As soon as the policeman saw him he shook his head. "You again?" he asked. "What's it this time?" A thief so well known by the police does not waste his energy protesting his innocence. He did not even try to deny my story and after a few harsh words from the law, he handed over my money to me. But my trips to Freetown were not only spent in catching thieves and avoiding trouble.

The Europeans had built a community outside of low- lying Freetown in a vain attempt to avoid catching malaria. It was known as Hill Station and was an airy, pleasant place on the hills outside Freetown where the Europeans isolated themselves in wooden houses built on stilts. When I arrived in Freetown this little community had been set up for some time.

One of the things I most enjoyed whenever I had some spare time was to watch the arrival of the white- hatted administrative officers at the railway station by the cotton tree. This railway line had been specially built from Hill Station to central Freetown to convey the European officials to and from their work. It was reputed to be the steepest non-funicular railway in existence, and as I was so interested in trains and hoped one day to be an engine driver, this particular line held great fascination for me. From the train the passengers were carried to their offices in hammocks.

My life was made much easier when the Smith family decided to move away from Kissy village to a house in Upper Kissy Road in Freetown. There was no more hurrying back and forth between village and town and I was able to spend more time with my classmates at my new school. This was Bethel School in Easton Street where Mr. McCormack, who was to become a well-known name in education, led us through the mysteries of Longman's Arithmetic, Nesfield's English Grammar and Prout's Hygiene.

During my time in Kissy and in Freetown, my father was always checking how I was getting on. He would pay us visits now and again and look me over to see how I was faring. I had known long ago at Moyamba, right at the start, that he was bent on making me 'sabi-book', as was my mother, although she wanted me to learn the Muslim book (the Koran), she herself being a Muslim; and she used to call me — and I still have memories of her voice — "Moi Siaka", which means Siaka the Muslim man.

When I returned home to my family for Christmas 1915, my school report showed that I was an average pupil and most of my family were impressed by the fact that I had reached Standard 4. But my father had higher ideals and asked me if I was really working hard enough. I replied that I was doing my best.

"Perhaps it is the fault of the school, then", he said, as if unwilling to admit that his son was not a genius! And so he made immediate arrangements for me to enter the Albert Academy in Freetown when the next term began on January 21 1916.

The Albert Academy was actually two years younger than

myself. It had been founded by the Evangelical United Brethren, who saw the need for a fee paying school offering a high standard of education to youngsters from the provinces. Some of the leading Creole families in the Colony, such as the Metzgers, who believed in integration with the up-country people, also sent their sons there rather than to the more fashionable fee-paying schools in Freetown. I felt very privileged to be going to such an exalted place of learning, and when I think now of how high the fees were I can only feel amazement at my father's determination to keep me there. It must have been a great sacrifice to him.

The two years that I had already spent in Kissy and Freetown had done something to rub off the rough edges of the country boy that I had brought with me to the big city. But it was only really when I attended the Albert Academy that I realized the real meaning of the word 'cosmopolitan'! There I was thrown in with Temne, Kono, Limba and Koranka boys — and boys from other Sierra Leonean tribes that I scarcely knew anything about. There were also students from Liberia, Nigeria and Ghana.

The social and tribal mix was tremendous, but strangely enough, unlike adults, we boys always settled our differences amicably and with good humor. We often teased each other about our different accents and dialects, but it was always good fun and no one ever took offence. I learnt that it was not how people say something, but what they say that really counts, and this was a valuable lesson for me.

I see now that if tribal and racial integration is to be successful then it should start at the cradle, as it did with me. And although loyalty is a fine quality, unqualified tribal loyalty can be a destructive force, within the framework of a free, multi-tribal country. Some people have never been able to grasp the difficulty of swallowing such loyalty; only a few years ago a tribe's very survival would have depended on the drumming up of a strong tribal feeling. Then suddenly, almost overnight, individuals were being told that this loyalty was wrong and what should be encouraged now was African nationalism — all very confusing.

And of course tradition dies hard and for many the ties of tribalism still seem greater than anything else. Often the bonds of tribalism lead to nepotism— something I have always disliked — and many an African leader has been vexed by this problem when filling key posts in his government. If he appears to favor one tribe more than another then he is heading for trouble. It is a wise and courageous man who picks his men according to their merit, and not because of their family allegiances. Africans must learn to accept their fellows for their own sakes if unity is to prosper in our continent.

Among the unifying factors which my friends and I at the Albert Academy had, and which kept us all together despite our ethnic mix, was hunger. It seemed that we could never get enough to satisfy our appetites, and for years it was as if I had a permanent aching hole in my stomach that needed constant filling. There were a number of mango trees in the school compound which, during the season, provided us with breakfast, for the school did not serve an early morning meal.

Some of us would be under the mango trees as early as 2 or 3 in the morning to pick up ripe mangoes which had fallen from the trees or partly eaten mangoes which had been dislodged by bats. These latter were named 'batmot'; we started eating the fruit where the bats had left off. The day the mango harvest finished was a very sad one for it meant that we had nothing to eat until the first meal was served at 11 a.m. Then we had to wait until 5 o'clock for the next meal — but even then my stomach was still rumbling for more food.

I shall never forget the way meals were served to us for the procedure caused me so much heartache. We would assemble in the dining hall, our ravenous appetites tantalized by the delicious smell of the cooking. The senior boys at each end of the table dished out the food while we, the youngsters, sat on benches at each side of the table eagerly awaiting our serving. But any hope we entertained of filling our bellies was soon shattered when, time and again, we witnessed the meagre portions allotted to us. The senior boy who served the rice used to sprinkle a little of it on a plate and then spread it out to create an impression of plenty.

When it was passed to his colleague to add the stew, he would put on the plate a mere spoonful of it which was sometimes little more than a practically meatless bone in a drop of gravy or a small sliver of fish stranded on a grain or two of rice. It amounted to so little that the whole helping could be swallowed in one gulp. The agony and resentment we felt were fanned to extremes when we watched how the seniors served themselves and each other. Their plates were stacked high with both rice and stew.

It was torture to watch those big louts stuffing themselves

with what seemed exaggerated relish while my own stomach was still so empty. But unlike Oliver Twist in Charles Dickens' famous book, not one of us dared to ask for more, nor to voice our bitterness in the mildest of terms, for they were far bigger than we were — and better nourished — and we feared reprisals. I do not think anything in adult life can ever compare with the torment of intimidation and humiliation quietly suffered by juniors in a boys' school who are completely at the mercy of the seniors. This painful transitional period, the half-way house between boyhood and manhood can sometimes change the whole character of a sensitive boy, and the change is not always for the best. But I was really very lucky because I had an uncle, Momo Kallon, who was a soldier and was stationed in Wilberforce barracks on the outskirts of Freetown.

Every Saturday I visited him and his wife, and a good meal was always assured! So once a week I would eat my till, with no senior boys nearby to cheat me out of my share. It was a wonderful sensation to feel as if I could eat no more, and as if this wasn't enough my kind aunt and uncle would always give me three pence to take back to school with me. With this money I would buy cupful of groundnuts at a halfpenny a time to tide me over the long hungry mornings of the school week.

This constant quest for food reached a fever pitch with an incident in which some of my friends were involved. Some boys stole vegetables from a nearby farm which belonged to the family of the late Pa Luke, once a foreman in the Public Works department. For some time the boys had been sneaking out at night and stealing cassava — and so far they had got away undetected. But their luck ran out one Sunday morning when we

51

returned from church having received the sacrament. Three of the boys went on ahead to the farm, and while they were busily digging up the cassava the Limba watchman caught them and insisted on taking them to his master. When the principal of the Academy, Professor D. E. Weidler, was told of their escapades he said "Take them along by all means, and don't spare the rod! Fancy stealing just after receiving the Holy Sacrament. What are boys coming to these days?" But the daughters of Pa Luke took pity on them and told the watchman to let them go. The boys were delighted at having got off so easily. But the next morning Dr. Weidler gave each offender a dozen strokes of the best!

About fifty per cent of the boys at the Albert Academy were called Mission Boys. Their parents could not afford the full fees, but as the boys were hard-working, well-behaved and showed promise, the school authorities felt they deserved help. The only difference between the Mission Boys and the rest of us was that in order to earn the supplementary money required for their fees, they worked for so many hours a day in the carpenter's and printer's shops. This meant that during some periods of the day they were working while we were studying. In spite of this advantage we had over them, it was nearly always the Mission Boys who came top of the class. The practical curriculum which was good for all of us, helped them in particular.

I was not long at the Albert Academy before I noticed that the different tribes have different idiosyncrasies of pronunciation. We found that the newly arrived Temne boys could not pronounce the letter 'J'. For example, they would say: *Kottoh Yames yam di koonoo a wan of yomp* which means in English- Big brother

James, bring the canoe alongside, I want to jump.

The proper rendering in Krio, of course, would be **Kottoh James, jam di kanoe a wan jompe**. We used to nearly to feel split our sides with laughter.

And then when it came to the Mendes, the aunt and pronunciation of the letter 'R' was anathema to them. Instead of saying with me rope they would say lope. Pronunciation of the word shun or the suffix -tion was always given as sun, for example, salvasun instead of, salvation. Every tribe had its own bugbear.

The Limbas put an 'F' wherever they found an 'H' and an 'H' wherever they found an 'F', thus foo-foo became hoo—hoo and hog became fog, whereas feel became Pa Luke, heel. We mocked one another a lot. I was later to realize that this same thing occurred even in the so far international field and I have met people of a big nation who, when they wanted to say rice say lice. So it is the same the world over.

Another incident of Academy days that stands out very clearly in my memory was the big influenza epidemic which fell on the city in 1918. One or two boys died in the school. As for myself, I lay down for a whole week just sleeping. I really do not know whether I should call it sleeping, it was more a sort of trance and I imagined myself walking.

When I was able to get up on a Saturday morning, I haltingly dragged myself along the streets of the city to Regent Road and on to Fourah Bay Road to visit my sister. I didn't come across a single human being on the streets. All I heard was the sound of hammering in the back yards where coffins were being made.

We were lucky in the Albert Academy to have the ministrations of one of our bishops (I think he was called Bishop Howard). He carried a small stove about in the dormitories where he boiled or steamed a mixture and made us cover our heads with our country cloths and inhale the vapor from the receptacle on the stove. This did wonders in clearing our nostrils right up into our heads. One of the symptoms of the epidemic as I remember it, was that one's nose got clogged up, then the head and the chest until eventually one succumbed.

My parents almost died of shock and worry when an itinerant unemployed man from Freetown, passing through Moyamba, called at our house and told my father, that almost all the children in the secondary schools in Freetown had succumbed to the plague. My mother even said that she had dreamt about this and had actually seen a ghost. Fortunately, after a few days real news reached them that I was still alive.

I often recall with amusement what happened that Saturday morning when I left the Albert Academy for Fourah Bay Road after recovering from my bout of influenza. When I arrived at my sister's, I found that she and the whole family with whom she was staying had just been laid low by the disease. At the same time I found that they had just finished preparing the usual Saturday foo-foo meal with the accompanying plasas — two big potfuls of it. Having been in bed for a whole week with scarcely anything to eat, you can imagine the effect all this food had on me. I sympathized with the family most heartily and then paid full attention to the meal. My sister lay down watching me while I voraciously helped myself. Now and again I would stop, drink a cup of water and sympathize with her. We were told at the time that it was a visiting man-of-war which had brought the plague to Freetown from the Far East.

The subjects that I studied at the Albert Academy were not as many as young people are required to study today, but were the basics, that is, reading, writing, arithmetic, composition, history, geography and a bit of Latin. I mention this matter because I have noticed in the case of one or two students whom I try to help along, lists for books in about fourteen subjects. I notice pupils in Standard 6 or Form 1 buying books on economics and other higher subjects. I do not profess to know how the principals or school boards draw up their book lists, but I should imagine that it would be better to get a good grounding in the basics before tackling the higher forms of learning.

Perhaps I should use this occasion to emphasize a point which has been very sore with me for a longtime, and that is the burden of the cost of books which parents have to bear. I feel quite certain that something can be done, and must be done, to relieve these parents. It is an unnecessary burden which they are called upon to shoulder while a few people enrich themselves in the process.

That is why, as President of Sierra Leone, I gave my support to a project designed to expand and modernize the Government Printing Press. The new equipment includes machines to rule and make exercise books and, as a result, we are now producing at least a very large proportion of the stationery used in our schools, saving foreign currency for the country and reducing the expenses of parents. We now also produce some text books.

Not so long ago I met one of our students recently returned from Russia and we were discussing the subject he had been studying. The pamphlet which he showed me on the subject was a cyclostyled one; in other words, cyclostyled copies had been made from the original text, and that is what he said his class used. Copyright laws do not make it possible for us to do that here, but I certainly know that the price parents have to meet could be halved, if not quartered, if both the writing and production of more text books took place in Sierra Leone. Somebody has gone so far as to say that our boys and girls here pay more for their books than the undergraduates in Oxford; and here there are only a very few libraries, whereas in Oxford or Cambridge there are libraries everywhere to help students.

On Thursday nights after school we used to go to prayer meetings in the E.U.B. Church in Regent Road. On Sunday evenings, too, we would attend the same church and we would enjoy the march along Regent Road. We certainly had some big men in school in those days because as we marched along the street we would hear some of the children shout: "Look dem big pa way day go school."

After school hours most of my time was taken up playing football. I was very keen and became pretty good at the game, for I was eventually picked for the school team to play regular matches against other secondary schools and Fourah Bay College. When I first started playing I was so small that the sleeves of my jersey covered my hands. This had its advantages for if I happened to handle the ball the referee rarely noticed it!

I remember, too, a football match we played against the Grammar School at the recreation grounds when one of our players, Kamara, a big hefty chap, charged a lean youth from the Grammar School and threw him violently to the ground. His uncle who was standing on the lines went and picked up the boy from the ground and said to him: "Cah we go home yah; mek den Mende pa ya nor kill you for me"

I might have grown equally fond of cricket had I not been put off the game by an accident that happened to me. I was playing long-stop for a very fast bowler. To help stop the ball and to protect myself from injury, I had a piece of board which I held over my forehead as soon as the ball had passed the batsman. On this occasion I mis-timed the ball and lowered the board just as it reached me. The result was a severe crack on my forehead which nearly knocked me unconscious. I decided there and then that this was not my sort of game and have never touched a cricket bat since.

One little amusement was to go 'pump riding'. There were huge pieces of flat stone in the bed of a little brook. So we used to go along and sit down and propel ourselves along the surface of the rock, heading downstream. It took quite a bit of dexterity to avoid danger but boys never think of things like that. We enjoyed it very much indeed.

Foreign troops who were stationed at Kortright, near where

Fourah Bay College now stands, used to provide us with a lot of fun. Some West Indian soldiers who used to wear long trousers and boots, would often roll past our school blind drunk helping to test our powers of mimicry as we tried to imitate their 'Bajan[3]' accent.

I remember once that four white soldiers got very tight and lost their way home. In their confusion they ended up in our school and accidentally entered one of the dormitories. Some of the boys, woken up by the noise, thought the soldiers where ghosts. A dreadful noise broke out as frightened schoolboys and drunken soldiers encountered each other, and eventually the police had to be brought in to escort the men out of the building.

The four terms corresponded to the four quarters of the year, with a short break after the first and third terms and a fortnight's break in the middle of the year. In December we had a long holiday of one month, so that all the boys could get home at least once a year to see their families. I can remember feeling like a tremendous man of the world whenever I met my old friends in Moyamba.

When we were about to go home, we, the freshers, were always supplied by some of the senior boys with a sheet of long English words for which we paid a considerable price out of our meagre pocket money. These were the words which we would use up-country to show the boys left behind that we had come from Freetown and had had some education. We would dress up in the morning and sit in a chair after having eaten a lot of cassava, and

---

[3] May refer to anything of or relating to Barbados

then begin to shout out a lot of big English words.

Young boys would collect around us, presenting a scene that resembled the old Greek orators lecturing. One such sentence for which I paid a penny (which was big money in those days) read something like this: "*Agitate the tintinabulary summons*", meaning:

Ring the bell". Or "*The conflagration extended its devastating career*", meaning in ordinary English: "The fire spread". The principal heard about some of these exploits of ours and on our return to school he would line up those found guilty and give them six strokes each. But we had satisfied ourselves and achieved our objective. The poor boys back home had a lot of specious regard for us, so we did not mind the punishment!

December was the official end of the school year, and it was then that graduation day was celebrated. For six years I had watched each generation of boys go onto the platform to receive their certificates. For some reason it seemed as if I would never walk that path, mount the few steps and be handed that important bit of paper it seemed such a distant attainment. But of course one day the time came for me to graduate from the Albert Academy. It came to me as quite a shock. I had become used to the protective walls of my school. I felt young and foolish and hardly able to cope with the demands of the real world. I kept asking myself anxiously: was I really equipped to leave school and earn my own living? Had I really learnt enough? Would I disgrace my family and teachers by the inadequacy of my knowledge?

My graduation day, my last day in the Albert Academy, was to be on December 1, 1922. Apart from my school fees, which were difficult enough for my father to find, I had to have special graduation clothes made and extra money for the festivities. In order to find the necessary money, my father had to send one of his wives, Mammie Nancy, to Freetown for a whole month to sell cupfuls of rice; and goodness knows what sacrifices he and the other members of my family must have made besides.

Nevertheless I know that, when I stood up to give my oration, it must have been a very satisfying moment for my parents who had both come down to Freetown. For my father it represented the answer to a prayer, the reward for years of hard work and self-denial. For as long as I live I shall never cease to be grateful to him for the opportunities he made possible for me by the sheer sweat of his labour and his great faith in me.

Knowing what importance my parents put on this very special day I could not help but feel nervous. Each graduating pupil was required to deliver an oration, and I had taken a lot of trouble in the preparation of my speech. The chairman of the occasion was the Governor of Sierra Leone, who had only recently been appointed. His name was Sir Alexander Slater and he was a strong critic of secondary schools in Freetown.

He believed that these schools neglected to train their pupils to use their hands and that they put too strong an emphasis on subjects like Latin and Greek. But our Freetown schools were very proud of their high standard of scholarship and learning and resented his suggestion that priority should be given to an industrial or manual education. Many Africans interpreted this to mean their activities should be limited to agricultural or general labouring, so that they would be kept forever as the labourers rather than the leaders of their own country. Not surprisingly, Sir Alexander was not a popular figure.

The subject of my oration was '**The Awakening of Africa**' and well I remember my final rousing sentences. I urged my fellow students to strive onwards— "Never look back until, like Caesar of old, you will be able to say 'Veni, Vidi, Vici' — 'I came, I saw, I conquered!'"

As I sat down, exhilarated as young men often are at their first taste of public speaking, I hoped that my parents were thinking to themselves that their sacrifice had all been worthwhile, and that I had made good use of my education.

The ceremony ended with the singing of our school song:

The golden glow of December's Day

Rests o'er the verdant hills,

And the sunlight falls with mellow ray

On fields and laughing rills.

But ere its last beams fade away

Beyond the mountains high,

Our lips must bravely say

The parting words — Goodbye.

Kind friends and parents gathered here

Our gratitude is yours

For all your care and sympathy

Which endlessly endures.

We trust the future may perfect

The works your hands have wrought,

And may they bring good gjfts to you

These years that swiftly fly.

When the graduation ceremony had finally ended my parents prepared a big dish of food which I shared with some of my friends. It was a very happy meal, all of us elated with the excitement of the busy day. We ate and ate until there was nothing left, and it seemed appropriate that after those first days of hunger when our tummies rumbled from dawn until dusk our school days should end on this note of plenty

Chapter 3
My First Job

When I left the Albert Academy, I was full of ambition. At that time, it was my hope that I would be able to continue my studies at the Lebanon Valley College in the United States of America. Of course, I knew that it was out of the question to expect my father to support me - he had already done all he could for me, and I was more than grateful - and so I was determined to work my passage to America and pay for college and living expenses as best I could by taking odd jobs. But the more I thought about it the more I realized that it would be selfish, and perhaps a little self-indulgent of me to further my studies.

I was seventeen years old and I had just finished the finest education as it was possible to have in those days in Sierra Leone. My father had worked and saved and made sacrifices so that I could go to the Academy and I considered that it was now my duty to find employment as soon as I could so that I in my turn could make some contribution towards the education of other members of my family.

Although I decided that this was the best path for me I still hoped that one day a chance for higher education would come my way. This hope was eventually rewarded in 1947 when I became a student at Ruskin College, Oxford.

I never cease to be amazed by the lengths that some Africans in the past have gone to in order to educate themselves, and when

I look around at students today I sometimes wonder whether they fully realize how very lucky they are now. It saddens me that so many of them take for granted the incredible opportunities open to them. Many seem to see a university degree as the rule rather than the exception: it is no longer their privilege to attend a college but a right. I am always amazed by the letters I receive from scholarship students complaining that the very generous grants that they receive are not sufficient.

They seem to think that cars, television sets and the very latest fashions form part of their proper dues. Yet I am not so old and unsympathetic that I am unable to identify myself with today's youth; had I been born half a century later I would probably be reacting in just the same way. There is nothing that youth does today that youth did not do in the past and I think the older generation should remember this and be tolerant. I know that when it is the turn of our young to shoulder the responsibilities of families, jobs, even of State, they will prove more than equal to the task.

My father probably had all the misgivings about me that we now have about our own children - after all, it is only natural that parents should want only the best for their offspring. Because he had been a soldier himself, he was always very anxious to see me in a uniform. He was certainly right to think that there can be no better training for a young man than a spell in the armed forces. The discipline and routine of service life, a kindling of respect for law and order and a sense of responsibility are valuable lessons for any young man. During the formative years of adolescence and early manhood there can be no better way of instilling a purpose in life.

However, before arrangements could be made for me to enlist in the Army, my father learnt that there was a vacancy in the Police Force for a sub-Inspector, and he urged me to apply.

"Of course, you can't expect to be made a sub-Inspector straight away, son," he said, but added optimistically. However, with your education it shouldn't be too long before you rise in the ranks."

I reported to the headquarters of the Sierra Leone police Force in Freetown in January, 1923. I must say that I did this more out of duty to my father than for my own pleasure, and certainly, life in the police force at first was very different from what I had expected. I had just reached the top of the ladder at the Academy, and now I found myself as a junior all over again.

The bottom rung is always rather a depressing place to be, but it is something that must be put up with and got through. Indeed, if I was to have any hopes of getting beyond this first position to more dizzy heights, I had to establish a firm foothold and prove my worth.

I'm afraid, though, that it is all too easy to be wise after the event; at the time I was young and in a hurry and itching to get on. As I stood in line with thirty or so other raw recruits to wait inspection I had already in my mind a picture of Sub-Inspector S.P. Stevens - complete with highly polished Sam Brown and baton. It was this vision that l kept myself at the front of my mind that kept me going during the exacting drill and fatigue duty that all junior policemen have to go through. After a while, however, my aching feet and general weariness overruled this splendid vision, and I had to face up to the day to day realities of my new life.

The Police Commissioner, Major C. Hampden King, was the best possible kind of tough guy - a disciplinarian of the old school. After our swearing in, he gave our group a talking to in his West Indian drawl. He told us, among other things, *'If you take anything like bribes or dashes or mass-mass while you are in the Police Force, you will be going to gaol as sure as God made Moses! You get me?"*

I can still hear his voice say it. It was a sound admonition. And I'm afraid that quite a few policemen did tend to land up in jail in those days.

The Police Force in those days was considered to be a place for illiterates and very few young men of secondary school caliber thought about it as a career. This was not so much because they were unattracted to the Force as such, but the truth was that those educated men who joined met with a lack of co-operation from the old hands that play on hostility.

Their lives were made miserable and their jobs difficult to do because of this obstructive attitude on the part of the illiterate element who would go to any length to safeguard their own positions even if this had a detrimental effect on the general efficiency of the Force. In my own case these old hands nearly succeeded in driving me out of the Police Force in those early days, and it was only the dread I had of disobeying my father that made me carry on.

Of course training was extremely rigorous and started at 6.30 a.m. with drill practice. At 8.15 a.m. we had fatigue duty for an hour where we had to clean up the officers' compounds and their kit and generally be at their beck and call. We would then have an hour of instruction in the duties of a policeman which would be followed until 11.30 by more drill until2 o'clock in the afternoon we would have a much needed break which would be followed by two hours of lessons in police duties. It was a tiring regime, and by 4 p.m. I was usually feeling pretty exhausted.

When I first joined the police there were no barracks and we stayed in various places in the city. This arrangement obviously had its difficulties, especially in the event of an emergency when the Force had to be gathered together very quickly. Commissioner King arranged for all policemen to move into King Tom Barracks which were situated a couple of miles from the centre of Freetown. This would have been at the end of 1923 – and the move was not as welcome as might have been anticipated.

The barracks occupied an area of land originally purchased by the British captain Thompson in May 1787 for the settlement of the first batch of freed slaves. Nearly 150 years later conditions there were not very much improved. The barracks had been left to rot since they had been last occupied by the artillery five years earlier. The buildings were in very poor shape, and had actually been condemned by the sanitary authority. Nevertheless' we were ordered to move in and make the best of it. It was not until

June, 1929, that the promised improvements were finally made and the place became for human habitation'

To report for duty-we had to march from King Tom to the Central Police Station one hour before we were due there'. The journey took about half an hour, we rested for 15 minutes' fell in and had General orders read to us and our beats allocated and then marched to our post. After the eight-hour spell of duty our day's work was over unless we had been selected for reserve duty, which meant reporting back to the station at 7 p.m. and sleeping there 'on call'.

My first assignment when I joined the Force was dog-catching. This meant that I had to go out two or three days at a time with two illiterate senior men to catch stray dogs, in the city of Freetown. Being the junior I was ordered to carry the empty sack. It was a *horrible business*.

Many of the dogs were in an appalling condition through neglect and were more often than not semi wild and vicious to handle. We had to aim to catch about three or four strays a trip, tie them in a bag and carry them back to headquarter, where they were locked up in a box which was fitted to the exhaust pipe of an old ambulance truck.

The engine of the truck was started and the dogs were suffocated by the Poisonous fumes from the exhaust. I suppose that if such a method of destroying life were used these days the police would find themselves in court but at least gassing was preferable to the method employed up to the previous year of drowning the poor beasts.

I remember once in Kissy Street we had caught four dogs in our bag and, as the weight was very -heavy, the policeman who was helping me to carry the load decided that we should put it down and rest for a while. As soon as we did, pandemonium broke out among the dogs trapped inside the bag and before we could do anything about it they had succeeded in getting loose. Understandably they were in an ugly mood and as we tried to recapture them they began to attack us from all sides. An excited crowd quickly gathered to watch, applaud and shout advice.

To take part in such an embarrassing spectacle even as an insignificant recruit, was humiliating enough, but the last straw for me was when a girl friend of mine from-Harford School in Moyamba,-who happened to be passing by at the time, suddenly recognized me. With a look of utter astonishment on her face, she, said: *"But I thought you were a police officer. What on earth are you doing chasing all those dogs?"*

We captured 422 dogs that year of which only 33 were lucky enough to be claimed by their owners. When l left the Force in 1930, although I was no longer employed as a dog-catcher thank goodness, 3,360 dogs, were bagged of which 3,140 had to be destroyed. In 1925 a new dog pound was built near King Jimmy, a part of Freetown, and a cart was provided to convey the animals instead of the abominable sack I had had to use, and the following year the Police Force employed two labourers to catch dogs which relieved us of this most distasteful duty.

An even more unpleasant memory I have was when I was asked to guard a corpse that had been washed up until arrangements could be made by the authorities to deal with the matter the following morning. The body was that of a lighterman[xiii] who had accidentally fallen into the sea two days earlier. I was terrified at the prospect of keeping it company until the morning. I had never seen a corpse before and the thought of death had rarely entered my head.

To make matters worse two days of being in the water made the body a gruesome sight. I tried to hide my fear when I asked the duty officer if I was to be alone with the body. "Unless you can get your grandmother to hold your hand!" he bawled at me.

There were no electric lights then and the Government Wharf was lit by two kerosene lamps which shed an eerie greenish glimmer on objects within their limited range, making them take on weird shapes. This played havoc with my imagination and at times throughout that endless night not only the covered mound of human remains, but many other objects that surrounded me seemed to move when I blinked my eyes and just at the moment when I stopped staring at them.' It was one the longest nights I can remember, but like most terrible night-time fears, in the morning it did not seem nearly so terrifying.

I was very lucky because promotion came fairly rapidly for me. Within a year I passed from full corporal with two stripes to acting sergeant with three stripes. At the end of my second year I was made first class sergeant which earned me £7.15s. (Le 15.50) a month. The strength of the Sierra Leone Police Force in 1923 was about 300 men. By far the most numerous tribe in the higher ranks were the Mendes, 78 per cent of whom were literate.

Of the Limbas, the third largest tribe in the country, there were only 15 and only three of us were literate. There were three divisions in the Force - A, B and C, each doing eight hours duty a day. I was drafted into B Division and sent out on the beat, patrolling the streets in eight-hourly shifts.' The most dangerous of the beats in Freetown were numbers 5 and 9 which comprised the areas around Soldier Fort and Hill Streets. These were frequented by night marauders and the police were often involved in unpleasant incidents.

To walk the streets for an eight-hour stretch could be a very tiring and soul-destroying exercise. To begin with it took a heavy toll on your feet. Police boots, until you got used to them and wore them in, could cause awful suffering. They were as heavy as lead. The uppers were thick and inflexible, the soles were studded and a thick steel plate was fixed to the heels for added protection. I remember the time I was on the beat in Kissy Road during the first few weeks of my patrol duty.

My boots were giving me such pain that I took refuge under what is now known as Over-the-Bridge near Eastern Police Station, removed my boots and rested my throbbing feet for a while. When I tried to get my boots back on it seemed a physical impossibility, so swollen had my feet become, and for the next hour or so I was hobbling like a cripple.

Chapter 4
Surviving the Depression

A policeman lives and works at the interface between the people and the impersonal authority. In a way, no job makes a better preparation for the responsibilities of government. I have always been glad, whenever I have had to make policy decisions or initiate legislation, that my work in the Force taught me to observe the effects of the law on ordinary men and women and see how it touched their needs and concerns. The policeman may be one of the humblest agents of the Executive but he can also be, for that very reason, among the wisest.

Fortunately, even after I left the Force, I stayed in jobs that kept me in touch with my people. My serious political initiation came only after a solid basis of life experience was laid, gradually broadening and diversifying among varying but always popular lines. The process was often tough and painful at the time - especially in the thirties, the years of world depression, when no rewards came easily - but I can say in retrospect that it helped give me enough maturity to see and do my duty, first as a trade unionist, then as a politician, but always as a representative of the people to whom I belonged, when the right time came.

After leaving the Police Force I was surprised to find how difficult it was to fit myself into civilian life. This was no fault of mine, for l was keen to take any sort of job that offered prospects, but unless there was a need for security men, most employers were somehow reluctant to place an ex-policeman among their staff. For several months, I drifted about doing odd jobs hoping for something good to turn up and feeling more and more despondent when it failed to do so.

If the future looked bleak for me, it certainly didn't for Sierra Leone whose financial prospects positively sparkled when a diamond was discovered in 1930 by the Geological Department in the Gbobora stream in Kono in the South-Eastern Province. It was the first of a rich deposit that was to be found scattered over some 480 square miles in the draining system of the Sewa River.

From that moment onwards the diamond area of Sierra Leone became the Mecca of all those believers in get-rich-quick miracles. The country was inundated — and still is — with fortune hunters from far and wide, illicit diamond diggers and dealers, smugglers and others, robbing the Government of thousands of pounds of revenue per annum. No matter how frequently raids are made to clear the area of strangers and illegal immigrants, however tight the security may appear to be, the racketeers persist, for police officers and security guards themselves, indeed even European employees of the mining company, have been found time and again unable to resist the temptation of stealing gems or conspiring with others to do so.

In view of the feelings of alienation and despondency I was going through when the first diamond was found in Kono, it is a wonder that I, too, was not prompted to join the diamond rush eastwards or the panners for gold along the river Makong where, since 1926, hopefuls defied fatigue and fever in their quest for a sizeable nugget. Somehow the idea of chasing rainbows has never appealed to me. It was always drilled into me both by my high principled father and at school, that there is precious little worth having in this life if you have not earned it the hard way. My feet were firmly planted on the ground, I expected to get my daily bread from the grindstone.

In 1930, the year when Sierra Leone was suddenly dazzled by the glitter of diamonds, other prospective mineral wealth also opened up new vistas to young men anxious to embark on a new career. Haematite iron ore[xiv] had already been discovered in two large hills near Marampa known as Massaboin and Gafal, 52 miles from the sea in the Port Loko district. Subsequent exploration confirmed that the deposits were promising but there was uncertainty as to whether the quantity and quality of the ore would justify development. It took a canny go-ahead Scot, James Campbell, to find out.

James Campbell, a member of the Northern Mercantile & Investment Corporation Ltd., of London, was a mining expert. Having satisfied himself that the deposits at Marampa justified development — and this in spite of the world depression of the early 1930's — his company, in conjunction with the experienced mining company of William Baird & Company, formed the Sierra Leone Development Company Ltd., (DELCO), in 1930.

Armed with the necessary mining rights from Government under the Concessions Ordinance, Campbell administered the kiss of life to the two comatose giants of Marampa. Before mining operations could begin, however, a 52-mile railway track had to be constructed to convey the heavy iron ore from its source near the small town of Lunsar to a loading port that it was planned to build at Pepel on the Rokel River where charting of the river had shown that ships of up to 100,000 tons could safely negotiate the channel.

The launching of the Marampa project quickened the heart-beat not only of the Colonial administration, the mining company concerned, investors, gamblers and all those who anticipated vast profits from the exercise, but also of one unemployed ex-policeman nearing the end of his reserves of hope, optimism and daily bread.

"I hear they're starting work on that Marampa-Pepel railway project at last", a friend happened to mention casually to me one day in October, 1930. I could not have moved faster had he suddenly gone berserk and chased me with a cutlass. There was no time for explanations. Here at last was the chance I had been waiting and hoping for and there was not a minute to lose.

I set out forthwith for Sahr Marank, which literally means *stone like an elephant* in the Temne language and juts out of a creek almost exactly half-way between the Marampa iron ore deposits and Pepel. It had suddenly become a booming settlement as a result of the company's decision to use it as its main base of operation with work on the future railway progressing simultaneously from Sahr Marank eastwards towards Marampa in one direction and towards the sea in the other.

As soon as I arrived in Sahr Marank, I presented myself as a prospective employee in whatever capacity they could find for me.

I gave details of my education and experience to the man in charge of recruitment. "Assistant clerk and telephone operator," he said, pointing to the door through which I must pass. "And make sure you arrive on time and do your job efficiently. We don't carry passengers here. Next one!" Without another word, he turned his attention to the next man in the queue.

There is, I was soon to discover, no nonsense in working for a contracting firm. Time was money. Every second had to be accounted for and any employee who failed to pull his weight was sacked at once. There was no room for sentiment between employer and employee any more than there would be between a government and a contracting firm if the company fell behind schedule or did a shoddy construction job.

There was no bargaining. You accepted the money offered and in return you were expected to do a good day's work. If you were above average there was no extra reward; if you were average you kept your job; if you were below standard you were very soon shown the door. Tough maybe, yet it is the only way to get a job done efficiently and, what is more, most men respect such treatment, for there is no doubt that a disciplined and orderly man is a happier, more productive and more progressive man.

Excuses are sometimes put forward that the average African worker is incapable of sustained hard labour because the diet he can afford to live on is way below the nutritional value he needs for expending such energy. This is certainly true to a degree, but as I see it, and from my own experience as an underfed worker at one time and another, the answer lies not so much in physical exhaustion through lack of calories, but in physical inertia induced by mental lethargy which is brought about by the uncaring and discouraging attitude shown by those in charge.

However hungry and underfed a worker may be, if he knows that his very livelihood depends on digging a hole, he will dig that hole in record time and still have enough reserve of energy to collect his reward.

Nothing so demeans men's dignity as the vicious spiral of dole and unemployment. Nothing is so enfeebling as a meaningless job which poses no challenge to a man. And nothing in the world of employment is so corrupting as excessive security, which destroys incentive and discourages effort.

In most of Africa today, a large public sector bears the brunt of the demands development makes on our emerging economies. Creating positive morale in the public sector work-force has therefore been a problem we have all had to face and it has not always been easy to combine high productivity with compassionate employment and welfare policies. Back in the 'thirties, although I had no experience myself as a government employee, many of my friends worked in various branches of the administration and were the butt of many ribald remarks about their cushy jobs, their regular increments and their come-a-day go-a- day attitude that over the years extinguished any spark of enthusiasm they once had.

It was the great difference in the attitude of government employees and that of the workers in DELCO towards their work

that struck me so forcibly when I first joined the Marampa
Railway Construction, as the project was commonly called. Most
of us were lean and hungry, some were visibly undernourished,
yet there was no question of easing up on the job however idly-
inclined or feeble we felt, for always uppermost in our minds was
the fear of being sacked.

It was tough in the extreme and many of us grumbled and
criticised and kicked against authority when authority was out of
earshot, as all workers do at times, but it made life simpler and
the job more secure if we disciplined ourselves to give maximum
co-operation, to do our best to see that the construction machine
of which we were an integral part ran smoothly on carefully oiled
wheels.

Discipline from the employer's point of view was particularly
necessary in the early 1930's, especially in the Protectorate where
labourers, whether local or otherwise, lived in close proximity
with the peasant population who were suffering such economic
hardship that the bitterness and unrest that emanated from them
could so easily have an adverse effect on the company's labour
force. There was still much resentment over payment of the Hut
Tax. Coupled with this, there was growing discontent over the
disparity of treatment of the Protectorate people vis-a-viz those
of the Colony, and the fact that what few imported goods there
were during that period of world depression rarely reached those
in greatest need of them, the masses of the hinterland.

It was clear to all of us at Marampa, employers and
employees alike, that the peasants were in the mood for rebellion,

though we did not view the matter in the same light. Whilst the company officials feared the repercussions such a rebellion might have among the workers on the project, we sympathized with the people, hoped for action and wished them every success. A bloody upheaval seemed near in February, 1931, when a Muslim visionary from French Guinea began interesting himself in politics rather than religion.

Haidara Contorfilli[xv], as he was called, had for past year been rather flamboyantly evangelizing the people in the Kambia District. He claimed he had been ordained by God "to prophesy about the prophecy of Mohammed". Kambia was just north of Port Loko District where we were working on the Marampa project and we heard many reports from time to time of his preaching. We found much of it amusing — the ravings of a religious fanatic, hysteria inspiring hilarity. Haidara claimed to have supernatural powers, to be able to change the sun into the moon, among other wonders, and he had an aversion to spinsterhood. "Give all unmarried women to husbands however the case maybe", he urged.

I personally never met Haidara, but those who had mostly agreed that he had extraordinary magnetism and, spoke with great conviction.

It was not difficult to understand how such a man, at such a time, could inspire and give hope to, and offer the necessary leadership to, an unenlightened community bent on improving their wretched living conditions at any cost. As the Colonial

Secretary of the day later assessed the position in the Sierra Leone Weekly News of February 21 st, 1931:

> *"The people must have complained to him of the hardness of the time due to the considerable fall in price of kernels and other staple products and their difficulty or inability to pay the tax... Some of the people readily believed and rejoiced that at last someone had come to rid them from the burden of taxation and acclaimed him an Angel of God."*

Nobody, not even the Provincial Commissioner in Kambia nor the Colonial Government, which declared him "illiterate and comparatively ignorant", took Haidara seriously. Not, that is, until February 10th, 1931. On that date he addressed a letter to his followers in Kambia urging them to revolt "God sends his messengers without guns or swords, staffs or daggers," he declared. "But he gives them something which is more than a gun or sword. I have the name of God with me; you should look at what is in the air, so you should not fear the European be he French or English, as the four corners of the earth are guarded by the Prophet Mohammed."

He told them that both their local Paramount Chief and the Government had fallen and that he had cursed everybody in the Government. "I am also telling you not to pay your House Tax to any Paramount Chief." He did not seem to be any too confident, however, about the reliability of the invisible and invincible arms to be provided by God to his messengers, for he distributed among his followers a generous supply of machetes and guns which must have been smuggled into the country.

It was obvious now, even to the British, that Haidara was intent on challenging authority and a platoon of 34 men of the Royal African Frontier Force was dispatched forthwith to put a stop to his rebellious uprising. The Colonial Secretary later explained to the Legislative Council Government's action in so doing:

> *"The Government is tolerant enough of empty, though foolish, talk, and was tolerant towards Haidara himself until it became clear that he was bullying the more ignorant people in the name of religion and openly preaching sedition and defiance of authority. But no Government worthy of the name would tolerate activities such as he adopted latterly, or would fail in its duty of taking strong measures against those who preach sedition, whether orally or by the written word."*

The army and the rebels came face to face on February 16th at Bubuya in the Northern Province. Among those killed in the brief but bloody encounter were Haidara himself and the British force commander.

As far as we on the Marampa Construction were concerned, the failure of the Haidara-led peasants to redress their grievances, sad as it was, showed clearly once more the futility of action by loose groups of people lacking organization and level-headed leadership against all- powerful authority.

We recognized that for the time being, until we organized ourselves into a trade union and were able effectively to fight for our rights and insist on fair play and fair pay through negotiations, the company must continue to have the first, last and only word. There was no alternative, things being the way they were. If we did not like their terms there was always a queue of job-hungry men only too ready to accept them.

At the peak of the Marampa Construction project there were about 5,000 men employed, including about 50 Europeans. It was possibly the last port and railway in Africa to be constructed entirely by hand labour with picks, shovels and head pans. Many of the Europeans were Scots who displayed the most incredible stamina in very trying circumstances. They were tough, energetic and diligent and they expected the rest of us on the site to be the same. There was no doubt that the example they set did much to spur on the whole project team.

I remember in particular the company's medical officer, Dr. A. A. McKelvie, a truly dedicated man who became so attached to Sahr Marank that after returning to Britain he wanted his ashes to be scattered over the site where he had spent so much of his energy. When he died and was cremated some years later, his relatives honoured his will sending to Sahr Marank the urn containing his ashes.

I found the broad brogue of some of them quite incomprehensible at first, likewise some of the English accents I heard, and I used to be amused at the badinage between the Scots and 'those Sasenachs', as they called their brothers south of the border, for I saw in it tribalism in its more sophisticated form, treated in the same light-hearted fashion as we had done as boys at the Albert Academy.

The Europeans lived on the work site which was at Sahr Marank near the Port Loko Creek Bridge. We, the African workers, stayed in Port Loko, three or four miles away, and had to trek to and from Sahr Marank each day. It was a strenuous schedule. Clocking-in time was 7 a.m. prompt, if we were as much as five minutes late we were sent home for the day and lost that day's pay. Work finished at 5 p.m., and by the time we had returned to our lodgings and had consumed our evening meal, we were usually too exhausted to do anything but go to bed and conserve our energy for the next day's work.

Still, I somehow found time to teach myself touch-typing and shorthand. There was a typewriter in my office which was seldom used and I thought it would be a good idea to acquire a new and useful skill. Somebody recommended a book in a 'teach yourself series and I sent for it. As soon as it arrived, I began to spend every minute of my spare time memorizing the position of letters on a standard keyboard, as reproduced in the book, and practicing the art of operating them with all ten fingers. Shorthand too became both a hobby and a challenge and I even wondered at times why people bothered to write in long hand what could so easily be recorded with just a few strokes of the pen.

I really enjoyed learning the techniques described in my book and what others thought was hard work I regarded as a sort of entertainment while the more conventional types of entertainment in which they indulged I tended to regard as a waste of time. Then, when I felt I had mastered the skills of typing and writing shorthand, I began to teach them to several clerks in the office. I have often wondered what exactly prompted me to do this.

I had never had the slightest ambition to be a teacher, and though I was conscientious where my job was concerned, I am sure that it was not the interests of DELCO that I had primarily at heart when I undertook to increase the work potential of their junior employees. I think, in retrospect, that it came as a natural reaction to me to help my fellow men share what little education I could impart to them when my own education had been so precious to me. After all, if you are starving and a bowl of food is put before you, you cannot greedily stuff yourself while others, equally hungry, look on.

The railway project was divided into two main sections, one stretching from Sahr Marank Bridge to Marampa, a distance of roughly 26 miles, and the other extending 26 miles in the opposite direction from Sahr Marank Bridge to Pepel; an engineer and an assistant were responsible for each section. In addition there were secondary sections, three on the Pepel site and two on the other. There were also two major bridges under construction, one at Sahr Marank, which I personally witnessed in all stages of development, and the other at Sankin Creek, about 5 miles from Pepel.

The track gauge of the railway, a single trace, was 3ft. 6in., and when the line was completed and in regular use, four or five trains each carrying around 1,800 tons of iron ore, were hauled to Pepel each day by coal-fired steam locomotives of around 130 tons in weight. Unlike the national railway, which proved such a drain on our economy that it was eventually phased out, the Marampa-Pepel railway has given valuable and efficient service throughout the 35-odd years of its active life.

While we were at Sahr Marank I used to go to Port Loko to collect mail about five miles up-river. We used a small boat with an outboard engine. Once on our way to Port Loko we saw an alligator lying on a huge stone on the side of the river with flies swarming all over its mouth. Not knowing anything about alligators, the launch skipper and I thought the creature was dead and decided to collect it, skin it and sell the hide. The skipper slowed the engine and steered for the rock where the alligator was basking in the sun. As soon as we got near the creature it gave a sudden jump which nearly capsized the boat. It was not dead at all, but very much alive, taking an afternoon nap and preparing to make a meal of the flies. It had very stale breath and I was told that when it opened its mouth the flies, thinking it was dead, congregated there; then, with one foul swoop, the alligator would snap its jaws and crunch as many flies as it could get. It was an unpleasant experience.

The Marampa Construction project came to an end in mid-1933 when the railway line from Marampa to Pepel was completed, and work on the iron ore mines was due to start later that year. We, the workers, expected to be immediately absorbed into the mining project, as the same company was to be in charge of operations, so we were very much taken aback when the whole lot of us were paid off. Luckily, I hung around in the vicinity for a month or so in anticipation of re-employment, and before long DELCO began recruiting, taking on one or two of us at a time.

I was offered the job of telephone operator at 2/- (20c.) a day. I objected strongly to this offer as I was earning 5/- (50c.) a day when I left the Marampa Construction. It was then explained to me that the reason why the firm had not absorbed us immediately into the mining project was because had they done so, they calculated that we would have expected to receive the same pay that we had been getting on the railway project. How canny can a Scot get?

It is, of course, only in retrospect that an ex-employee can appreciate the tight shoestring that DELCO had to operate on. Even after the mine became fully operative the margin of profits was very slim, for so many hands had to be employed both in the construction of the railway and port and in mining operations on account of the labour being entirely manual. In the early years, iron ore was being delivered to Europe, chiefly the United Kingdom and Germany, for around 15/- (Le 1.50) per ton.

Out of that the company had to reimburse itself for the cost of mining, railway freight, loading the ship and ocean freight charges which were then about 8/- (80c.) per ton. At the same time, however, the question of the company's profit or loss concerned me less than the rough deal I considered had been given me. I was most reluctant to accept such a drop in salary when it meant doing the same job for the same company after two years of satisfactory service. But the alternative was to return to Freetown and join the ranks of the unemployed, which was even less attractive. So I signed on.

Work on this new mine was almost like the beginning of the construction work at Sahr Marank in 1930. We were living in Lunsar, about 2 miles from the works on the iron ore hill, Massaboin, and had to be on duty when the siren sounded at 7 a.m. The hill was inhabited by baboons which very often crossed our path. These large apes can be very dangerous if they are in a bad mood, if they are taken unawares or protecting their young. When blasting operations began at the mine they gradually dispersed and took refuge in other parts of the hill, which made our daily trek less hazardous.

Although I was employed as telephone operator and private secretary to the general manager, I soon found that when you are working on a newly opened mine under hardy Scots you can be called upon to do all sorts of jobs far removed from the one for which you were hired.

One day it was announced that the Governor, Sir Arnold Hodson, was going to visit the mine. All hands were mobilized into making the site as smart as possible in honour of this august personage. I was plucked from my switchboard, given twenty labourers and told to supervise the construction of a small road. After we had finished building the road, I noticed that it was a bit wet in places. Anxious to make a smart job of it, I looked around for some means of correcting this defect and my eyes alighted on a pile of sand conveniently heaped nearby. It was ideal for what I had in mind and I told the labourers to shovel it onto the wet spots to soak up the moisture.

Our general manager, a Scot six and a half feet tall, arrived to inspect the road. Instead of admiring our handiwork he went into a fit of rage. "What the blazes d'ye mean by scattering that valuable sand all over the damned place? Did ye no' ken that it was brought up here at great cost for a special job?" This unexpected censure was humiliating enough, but when I was told that I would have to refund the cost of the sand my dejection sunk to unfathomable depths.

Not all my odd jobs on the Marampa mine project had such unhappy endings, I am glad to say. When the engine parts arrived from overseas and had been assembled, and the railway was about to be put into operation, the question arose as to who would take on the job of station master. The difficulty was that the engine drivers were all European and the management were most reluctant to appoint an African as station master because it meant he would have to give instructions to the drivers. Such a reversal of roles in the established white master-black servant relationship would *never* do! However, after much discussion it was found that there was simply no choice in the matter.

The post would have to be filled by an African. Whether I appeared to the management to be the least likely to take advantage of my exalted position, or whether my passion for railway engines radiated so strongly from my person that they were attracted to me as if by a magnet, I never knew. But the fact is I was offered the job and so became the **first station master — of any race** — on the Marampa-Pepel railway.

The railway worked on a system of its own and there was only one stationmaster. The system was called 'no signalman token'. After Marampa, there were three stops before Pepel. A loaded train on leaving Marampa was given a token or key by the station master after shunting processes had been completed. With this token on the engine, the train went into the main line at each stop, or loop, as it was called.

It could not get out of the loop without certain operations. If it tried to do so it would be derailed. On arriving in the loop, say the first loop, for example, the driver would go into the token box and deposit the token with which he had travelled from, say, Marampa. If the forward section of the line was clear, the station master at Marampa would give the driver permission to withdraw the token for that section. The driver would then turn a nut on the instrument linked up to that section and he would be able to extract the token.

If the forward section was engaged, he would not be able to extract the token for that section. If the forward section was clear and he had been able to extract his token, he would then walk along the railway to a point before the engine and with the token he would operate a lever which opened the way for the train to move out of the loop. He would then go back to his engine and drive the train out of the loop.

When the last truck cleared the lever which he had operated, the lever would again be reversed and locked. Upon being locked the points would then be set for the siding (not the main line). The driver could then take his train to the next stop. It was a bit of a slow process, but since it was a freight train, there was no special hurry and, under the system, accidents such as trains coming into collision, just could not happen. Of course trains did come off the rails now and again, but that was not due to anything like traffic collisions.

As station master I sometimes worked until eleven at night, then came back about three or four in the morning. During slack, or slacker periods, I also taught myself the Morse code then used to transmit messages and telegrams between Marampa, Pepel and Freetown. This was a slow and cumbersome system which, unlike the telephone introduced some years later, required trained operators. However, as station master, I felt that I should not have to rely entirely on the operators and that I should be able to cope in an emergency.

Again, a 'teach yourself book helped achieve my purpose and eventually I became so familiar with Morse that I began to teach it to trainee operators at the station. The messages we used to send were many and varied and were not confined to tonnages and shipments. "Arriving yours about 8.30 a.m. tomorrow," the cashier at Sahn Marank advised his counterpart in Pepel, adding: "If you will invite me to breakfast I shall be pleased to accept."

All this kept me so busy in my station master job that some nights I never went home. At the peak period we ran as many as seven trains a day. When the trains arrived at Pepel the wagons were emptied by mechanical process, one at a time, onto conveyor belts which moved the ore to a stockpile at the port. Underneath the stockpile there were valves which, when operated, dropped the ore through a regulated opening onto other conveyor belts which travelled out to the loading installations and loaded the ore into steamers. By this process huge ships of 40,000 or 50,000 tons could be loaded in a few hours.

The ore mined at Marampa was obtained by open cast methods and consisted of big pieces of rock which were blasted into smaller pieces. These were sorted, loaded into mine tubs and dropped into railway wagons to be hauled to Pepel for shipment. The first ship to be loaded at Pepel in September, 1933, was the *S.S Hindpool of* 5,000 tons, which carried lump ore to Glasgow. In contrast, when I visited Pepel in 1972, I saw berthed there a vessel of 100,000 tons which took not more than eight or nine hours to load — I then heard that 2½ milion tons of concentrates, that is, treated fine powder ore, were exported in 1971.

This powder ore, which was found underneath the capping of red ore, had an iron content too low to warrant shipping in its natural condition and was therefore passed through a special mill which produced from it a concentrated product of around 66 per cent iron content.

Marampa was then one of the most up-to-date iron ore mines in the world. Accommodation was provided for both European and African employees; there were hospital, educational and canteen facilities, a club and, welfare centre, a swimming pool, tennis court, cricket pitch and other recreational opportunities. Above all the management was actively concerned with the prevention of accidents. In the early stages of the mining there were a lot of accidents caused mostly by the weakness of an endless rope gravity haulage system.

Loaded tubs being hauled by this contrivance en route to the railway wagons or the washing and screening plant would sometimes cut loose and come hurtling down to the loading platforms at terrific speed, more often than not killing or maiming a number of workers who were unable to get out of the way in time. To the management these were 'regrettable' accidents calling for *a stereotype* expression of official condolences, coupled with a minimal monetary grant to the bereaved families.

Unable to conceive the possibility of safety devices, such as those which were to be generally introduced in the mining industry some 20 years later, the workers came to accept these tragedies as inevitable occupational hazards, the price one occasionally had to pay for the privilege of a meagre but regular wage. To the survivors, "one" was naturally somebody else and, human nature being eternally optimistic, few were those who took seriously the risk of losing their own lives.

To the families of the victims, however, it was a different story. Wives, children, brothers and sisters, could hardly control their grief when news of a fatal accident affecting a husband, a father, or a close relative reached them. They would rush to the mine from far and near, the muscles of their legs apparently stimulated by sorrow and despair. Still oblivious to fatigue, hunger or thirst, some eventually broke down as they approached the body of the deceased.

The immensity of the shock brought about by the loss of a dear parent came home to me once again in those days when I too was struck by a personal tragedy. Late on Good Friday 1941 the shattering news reached me that my father 'as critically ill in Moyamba. My step mother had arrived a few days earlier in Lunsar to spend a holiday with me. We instantly decided to go home as soon as possible and took the road to Moyamba early on the following day.

Naturally, we had to rely on our feet and stamina to reach our destination in time to see the old man alive. We walked throughout Saturday and Sunday, stopping only from time to time for a drink of water, a bite of food, and to cross the Rokel River by canoe. When we arrived at Moyamba on Sunday evening, Easter Sunday, my father was already in a coma and died before the end of the day.

I had been deeply saddened when I lost my dear mother the very year I joined the Police Force and home had never been quite the same without her there. The loss of my father, however, was a very real tragedy to me. It was he who kept alive the flame of endeavor within me, who inspired me and gave me hope, who never allowed me to despair when things did not work out as well as I had hoped they would.

To please him and earn his pride was the focal point of every venture and his death seemed to rob me of that purpose.

Unlike my mother whose body was returned to her homeland for burial, my father's body, lying on the left side according to Limba custom, was laid to rest in Moyamba, his adopted home where he had spent so many years of his life and where he was an active member of the United Methodist Church.

Towards the end of my career at Marampa, I was eventually able to make some practical use of the initiatives I had taken in learning typing, shorthand and other office techniques. World War II was now raging in Europe, North Africa and the Far East and our European employees were naturally most interested in its progress.

One of them was assigned the task of monitoring BBC news broadcasts — that is tuning in to the BBC on short waves — and typing out a news sheet for distribution within the company, a sort of miniature newspaper which became the only source of information for the expatriate Britons isolated in a small mining town in West Africa to supply iron ore for the Allied war effort. As fate would have it, the European 'editor' of our newspaper became ill and, as I was presumably the only other man in the company able to write shorthand, I was given the job of producing the news bulletin.

This involved transferring me from the railway station to the main office with the grade of senior clerk and a salary of 200 per annum which made me one of the company's highest paid African employees. It also enabled me to follow current world events in much greater detail than I would have done as a station master and thus to develop an interest in, and understanding of, foreign affairs. This background knowledge proved of some use when I began to take an active part in politics and government.

Apart from one or two serious strikes that took place during the life of the Marampa iron ore mines, the project did continue to run on the solid no-nonsense lines that its Scottish founders laid. Unfortunately, neither this conservative approach to industrial relations nor the devotion, sacrifices and hard work of employees, both African and European, could make up for the failure of management, over the years, to re-invest in the mine a sufficient proportion of their profits in order to modernize production and make it more competitive.

By 1976, the slump in the world iron ore market, coupled with the exhaustion of the richest and most accessible deposits, brought about the closure of the whole operation, putting out of action a sizeable infrastructure, including a port and railway, and making redundant thousands of Sierra Leonean workers in a country already suffering from unemployment.

As a result, Lunsar, which owed much of its development to the operation of the Marampa mine, became almost a ghost city, though the Government did what it could to mitigate the situation.

At about the same time, some 200 miles away, in Western Liberia, a similar fate struck the town of Bomi Hill where, in less than 25 years, an American company managed to remove to the United States a mile- high mountain of iron ore, leaving in its place a huge crater surrounded by a mass of abandoned installations and infrastructure and an army of unemployed workers.

In a way these experiences are typical of old-fashioned capitalist enterprise in colonies and underdeveloped countries. The quest for quick profits brings about a sudden inflow of capital together with the dislocation of traditional patterns and profound changes in the social and physical environment. Boom towns appear almost overnight, their bright lights and the prospect of a regular money income, however meagre, attracting tens of thousands of farmers who leave their villages to swell the ranks of the urban proletariat.

Then, when the richest pickings have been exhausted, or market conditions change, the investors just leave the country without much concern for the social, economic and political havoc they may leave behind, and the human suffering their activities may have caused. The villagers who took the one-way road to wage-earning will have spent much of their working lives in the employment of the company. Few, if any, will ever return to their farms to grow the food so badly needed by their families and their fellow countrymen at large.

Lest these remarks should be interpreted as a general condemnation of foreign investments in developing countries, I should make it clear in the first place that my reflections on this subject refer mainly to the exploitation of finite or wasting assets, particularly in such areas as mining and forestry and, to a smaller extent, fishing. In the second place, I am glad to observe a new, progressive tendency on the part of responsible investors to take a longer-term view of their association with the country in which they operate and to adopt policies designed to safeguard not only the environment and the welfare of the people whose lives have been directly and irreversibly affected by the investment, but also the future interests of their own shareholders.

In forestry, it is now common practice to expect concessionaires to replant trees at least at the rate at which they take them away. Some have even shown sufficient foresight to replenish the forest with species which would provide the raw material for the development of local industries, such as Indian Malina trees used for making paper pulp.

In the mineral sector, while some companies still make a quick getaway after skimming the cream of a deposit and amortizing their initial investment many times over, other companies re-invest part of their profits in the country, either in modern equipment designed to make viable the exploitation of poorer quality ores, or in other areas such as industry and agriculture. At the same time they also train their employees to make a living in a variety of occupations unconnected with mining.

Thus, in the neighboring country of Liberia, the largest of the iron ore mining concerns, after exhausting the direct shipment ore (ore which can be fed directly into furnaces) has invested millions in plant to beneficiate and pelletize the lower grade ores. The same company has also embarked on a 'spin off' program of local agricultural development and the re-training of workers in anticipation of the day when they will have to find alternative means of livelihood.

At Marampa it was perhaps our good fortune that DELCO decided to wind up their operations long before exhausting the potential of the deposits. This has given us the chance to negotiate new agreements with more forward looking investors who would take full advantage of modern technology and would also show more consideration for the future of their employees.

Naturally, the re-opening of the Marampa mine would also constitute a useful source of revenue for the Government. A heavy hunk of iron ore is not an easy or desirable commodity to hide on one's person and smuggle out of the country, and unless you hoard a ton or two of it, even if you could find a ready buyer, the price offered would never compensate for the trouble taken in amassing it. So every ton of iron ore mined is revenue for the mining company and the Government of Sierra Leone.

This is not true of the more valuable revenue-earner on the opposite side of the country, the diamond mining area of Kono, where it is estimated that the money lost to the country through illicit diamond digging and smuggling has run into millions of pounds. Small-scale mining started in Kono in 1933; two years later a private expatriate firm, the Sierra Leone Selection Trust, obtained exclusive prospecting and mining rights for virtually the whole of Sierra Leone. In spite of their rigid security measures, it was found to be impossible to stem the flow of humanity hell-bent on discovering a priceless gem in the dirt and gravel of a river bed.

Not only the unemployed and foreigners joined the ranks of fortune hunters, but people in steady jobs such as teachers and clerks resigned their positions of security to gamble with their fate. Farmers left their crops unattended to join the stampede, which resulted in an acute shortage of rice and other vital foodstuffs, causing prices to rise beyond the reach of most of the workers.

Living conditions in the mining area were appalling: too many people, too few houses, no sanitation and little food. In this squalor the fight for survival and the lust for diamonds became a cut-throat business. Forty-five murders were recorded in the area in 1954 and in one case a mob of gangsters killed and disemboweled a man to possess a diamond he had swallowed for safe-keeping.

I had recently been made the first Minister of Lands, Mines and Labour at this time, so I was acutely concerned with the explosive state of affairs in the Kono district. I realized that it would be incredibly difficult, if not impossible, to rid the area of illicit diggers and the only answer as I saw it was to organize them on an official basis by issuing licenses to diggers. If this were done, those with licenses would be only too keen to fence off their allotted area against illicit diggers, and if it were also arranged for them to sell through a government buying organization which gave as good a price as could be had across the Liberian border, this would discourage smuggling and guarantee revenue for the country that at that time 'was being lost altogether.

I believed that unless prompt action were taken by the Government to allow the people of the country substantial participation in the mining of diamonds, the whole situation would get out of hand and we would be faced with epidemics, riots and bloodshed of a most serious nature. I was even more convinced that this was the only course to take on my return from a visit I made to the diamond mines in the Gold Coast.

The Sierra Leone Selection Trust did not take kindly to the idea of licensed diggers and the negotiations entered into on the subject between that company and the Government in January, 1955, ended in stalemate. Talks were resumed in London on June 27th and I was a member of the delegation, led by the Chief Minister, Dr. Margai, which travelled to England to take part in these discussions.

Agreement was reached in principle, but trouble arose over the amount of compensation to be paid to S.L.S.T., who were asking the unreasonable figure of £10,000,000. Dr. Margai returned to Sierra Leone and left me and his brother, Albert, to battle on. I spent almost three months in London before the company finally agreed to accept £1,570,000.

They were tedious weeks indeed for one way and another Albert Margai and I failed to manage on the per diem allowances made to us and more often than not we could not even afford the bus fare from the Regent Palace Hotel in Piccadilly where we were staying to the Colonial Office in Victoria, and had to walk.

*I worked hard both physically and mentally to save the
country nearly nine million pounds and felt very nettled when
complaints were registered on my return that the sum agreed
was too high!*

The agreement made with S.L.S.T. in 1955 reduced their exclusive rights to an area *of 450* square miles in the Kono district and in Lower Bambara Chiefdom and Kenema districts. All rights in the rest of the country were surrendered to the Government and a scheme for licensed digging in those government controlled areas was set in motion and was known as the Alluvial Diamond Mining Scheme. The first license, at a cost of £9 a year or £5 for a half year, was issued in Lubu Chiefdom, Bo District on February 6th, *1956,* and by the end of March, 1,500 licenses had been granted.

In addition, the licensed diggers were required to pay rent of 4/- a week to the Tribal Authorities. Similarly, Government arranged to buy diamonds from the licensed diggers. On February 7th I opened the main buying offices at Bo and soon after the opening ceremony diamonds were bought to the value of around £2,000. Later that month a second office was opened in Kenema. Valuers also trekked through the bush to contact diggers in the outlying districts and bought stones on the spot.

In addition, the scheme provided for licensed dealers to cover the vast mining area. A dealer's license cost £25 but it could be issued to a man of any nationality or race, unlike the digger's license which was issued to Sierra Leoneans only.

The majority of diamonds found in Sierra Leone are of gem quality and average between two and three carats. But in January of 1945 one of the largest alluvial diamonds in the world was discovered in the Woyie River in Kono weighing 770 carats. Called the Woyie River, it was sold for Le500,000 (£250,000).

On February 14, 1972, the third largest gem diamond ever found was recovered in the Company's Separator House at Yengema from concentrates sent in by No. 11 Heavy Media Plant. It weighed 969.1 carats, nearly half a pound, and measured roughly 2½" by 1½", slightly larger than a hen's egg.

I named it 'The Star of Sierra Leone', and it was recently sold for several million dollars. It was most fortunate that this diamond was found legally in the Company's Separator House. If it had been found by independent miners, passed to illicit dealers and smuggled out of the country, not only would Sierra Leone be a lot poorer financially, but the credit due to her for this record find would have been lost.

Both iron ore and diamonds are wasting assets and for many years the audited profits of neither DELCO nor SLST were published, so that Sierra Leone derived tax only from what the two exploiting companies declared to us as profits on their yearly output. It has always been my view, and I have made no secret of it, that any country blessed with mineral deposits or any other form of potential wealth should have a controlling interest in the management as well as at least an equal share in the income earned.

When I became Prime Minister in 1968 I at once sought to clarify my Government's policy with regard to the mining companies by addressing the Sierra Leone Chamber of Mines as follows:

> "I have asked to meet you because I understand that there is some apprehension in the Mining Industry and its ancillaries in regard to the policies of the new Government in so far as these policies will affect the industry.
>
> "On behalf of my Government, I should like to say that we have no plans to change the operational policy of the mines now or in the immediate future. No one realizes more than we do, the vital part which the Mining Industry plays in the economy of Sierra Leone and it is not our intention to do anything which will jeopardize the life of the 'goose that lays the golden eggs'.

What we think any responsible new Government would do and what the people of this country expect us to do, is to examine closely every aspect of the industry so as to make certain that this country is getting the maximum financial benefits out of the mining operations, bearing in mind that the life of the mines is limited and taking into consideration the country's serious financial situation, not to mention the need for money for development.

For example, we intend to find out if we cannot share with the mining companies the financial benefits which should accrue to them as a result of devaluation. We intend to find out whether the eight year tax holiday which one of your companies is to enjoy conforms with the general principles of mining agreements in other parts of the world.

We should also like to find out the precise basis for the calculation of the profits of which 50-60 per cent are supposed to be reserved for our benefit by some of the mining companies." Although there was at that time a Sierra Leonean on the Board of the Sierra Leone Selection Trust, and our Government netted around 70 per cent of the company's profits through the Diamond Industries Profit Tax and Income Tax, I was not satisfied, upon examination, that the country was getting the maximum financial benefit from the Mining Industry and that, indeed, it never would unless and until it became a major shareholder in the enterprise.

In December, 1970, therefore, my Government acquired 51 per cent of the SLST shares and the company was renamed the National Diamond Mining Company of Sierra Leone Limited (DIMINCO). It was recently pointed out to me that since the formation of DIMINCO an increasing number of large diamonds are being found in the Separator House in Yengema. Part of this may be due to my Government's action in driving from the mining area all so—called 'strangers', that is, those found guilty of not being in possession of non- citizen Registration Certificates, of entering Sierra Leone without travel documents and of being in the diamond protected areas without Residential Permits.

At the Separator House the threat from thieving is the most dangerous because the diamonds are easily selected there within a short time. It is one thing to steal at the plant sites and from the dumps where one has to do a lot of washing of gravel before getting the diamonds, and another thing to steal from the Separator House where gems, cleaned and sorted, are more or less offered on a plate.

This alone proves how important it is for us to participate in the mining of our mineral resources and I strongly feel that any future agreement between our Government and a company wishing to re-open the Marampa mine will have to provide for the operation to be conducted on a partnership basis between us. Such partnership agreements should have been drawn up, financed and put into effect at the time of Sierra Leone's independence in 1961, when the country officially came of age and was allowed to control its own affairs. Without such active participation, neither the exploiting companies nor the exploited country concerned can respect one another and operate the mines so that the maximum productivity is achieved for the benefit of both partners.

> My Government is going all out to get the indigenous people involved in our economic development, for it is shameful to have to admit that today, over 20 years after gaining our political independence, something like 70 to 80 per cent of the economic activity of the country is in the hands of foreigners.

Of course we realize that we cannot legislate people into business. There has to be training and a certain amount of aptitude, and a willingness for sustained hard work. We realize, too, that there is a great need for outside capital and technical know-how, both of which we wish to encourage in every possible way. It is vital that we concentrate on our economic development, for I strongly believe that it is this which puts flesh and blood on the skeleton of political development.

Chapter 5
A Study Period in Oxford and London

Shortly after the publication of the 1947 Constitutional Proposals, I was absent from Sierra Leone for 18 months or more. Edgar Parry, the British Labour Adviser, who had taken a great interest in my trade union activities, suggested that I might try for a British Council scholarship to study industrial relations at Ruskin College in Oxford, and later undergo a six months' training course run by the Trades Union Congress in Clapham, which involved attending union meetings, working in union branch offices and visiting mines.

Naturally I was delighted with the chance this would give me of increasing my knowledge and generally broadening my outlook so that I would be better equipped to deal with the political work in which I was becoming increasingly involved. Fortunately, I was awarded this scholarship and late in 1947 I set sail from Freetown for Liverpool.

As the ship sailed northwards and the blue seas and warm sunny days gradually gave way to strong north-easterly gales and black skies, I began to doubt the wisdom of my journey into foreign parts. I was apprehensive about how I would get on with my fellow students. In Africa, almost all white people looked down on Africans, keeping themselves aloof from us and going about in our midst with an Arch- angelic air of superiority. In the workshop, in the office, no matter where, whenever issues cropped up in which an African was pitched against a European, the conclusion was a foregone one: the European could never be wrong. Like the Pope, he was believed to be infallible. Europeans who did try to befriend us did so at their own peril. Such fraternizers were regarded by their compatriots as having let the side down. At the very least they could expect to be ostracized and have their names taken off the membership list of The Club, but the more usual treatment was an abrupt departure, a one-way ticket home for what was called 'leave prior to retirement'.

In the mind of the average colonial European, socialism was not for export, colonial affairs were not party politics. Socialists, trade unionists, conservatives, no matter what banner they travelled under, they were all the same in their dealings with us.

So one can imagine the trend of my thoughts when on entering Ruskin College in January, 1948, I found myself one of two West Africans amongst a host of European men and women.

Ruskin College was founded in 1899 to provide working men and women with opportunities for full-time education and was the first residential college for adult education to be established in Britain. I lived in an extension of the College called The Rookery, a beautiful old house in Headington, parts of which dated back to Tudor times, which had only that year been purchased by Ruskin to accommodate forty students.

I must admit that I was greeted on arrival in a most friendly and welcoming manner both by my fellow students and the members of the staff, but in view of my experience of Europeans in Africa, I doubted their sincerity. Politely but stiffly I acknowledged their handshakes, then lit my pipe and blew out a cloud of smoke, partly to cool my nerves and partly to establish a screen behind which I could take stock of my colleagues without appearing to stare at them. They were a lively lot and although they were as strange to one another as they were to me, I noticed that they were already on first-name terms. Before I knew it I found myself the centre of a group of white faces, all eager to introduce themselves and to learn my christian name.

Within minutes, the warmth that emanated from them began to penetrate my smoke screen and melt my defensive shield, and to my great surprise, I felt the tension within me relax as I naturally responded to the atmosphere of cordiality and helpfulness that is found only among genuine friends. Effortlessly they drew me out of my self-imposed isolation and treated me as one of themselves.

My all too brief sojourn in Ruskin College was one of the happiest periods of my life. From the Principal, with his rich, sonorous voice, his ready availability at all times and his willingness to help, right through the whole staff, all were so tactful and gracious, and never once was there any suspicion of condescension in their attitude towards me as an African. The student body — Englishmen, Scotsmen, Welshmen, Irishmen and Americans — the whole lot were wonderful companions.

Communists and fellow travelers seized every opportunity to discuss the grand millennium when the workers would rule the world. Socialists were always advocating hastening slowly, and so on. They taught me how not to go to bed before one in the morning, how to hurry for a second helping at table, how to make do with little and how to develop a taste for kippers[4] which I sprinkled with cayenne pepper and cooked over a gas ring.

The only occasion when I nearly came to blows was with a Scotsman who shared my room and who insisted on the window being kept wide open each night whatever the weather. As soon as he opened it I got out of bed and closed it. Grumbling, he got up and opened it again, then I, my temper visibly rising, slammed it shut. One night after this had been going on for some time we met in the middle of the floor like two fighting cocks, each one waiting for the other to show his spurs. Suddenly the stupidity of the whole thing hit me and I withdrew.

I realized that the cold icy air was as vital to that hardy Scot as the African sun was to me and I was, after all, a guest in his country. That winter of 1947 was the coldest the British could remember. I shall never forget my horror one morning when I gripped the chrome handlebars of my bicycle with my gloveless hands and found they had stuck!

It was not only among the students and staff at Ruskin that I met this spontaneous acceptance and kindliness. The country was suffering acutely from post-war depression with the accent on queues and ration books. Food was scarce and both

---

[4] A **kipper** is a whole herring, a small, oily fish, that has been split in butterfly fashion from tail to head along the dorsal ridge, gutted, salted or pickled, and cold smoked over smouldering woodchips (typically oak).

housewives and shopkeepers were harassed by the problem of making a little go a long way.

My meat ration, the butcher told me, was two pounds a month. "I'll take two pounds of beef," I told him as I counted out my money. He stared at me with astonishment, "Well, as yer like," he said, shrugging his shoulders, "but don't come back next week, mind, and expect to get any more. That there's yer month's ration, mate." I stewed the whole lot and ate it.

The following Saturday I again tagged on the end of the queue. "Ere you!" he called, catching sight of my black face, "I reckon I told yer..." I looked at him innocently and hungrily, smiled and winked, but kept my place in the queue. When my turn came he disappeared behind the scenes and returned a few minutes later with a newspaper bundle which he put in my hands. "Just this once, then," he said. "But remember, mate — no more till next month. Yer'll get me wrong, yer will."

The whole time I was in England I was regularly served with two pounds of beef a week. I could well have understood it if I, so obviously a stranger, had been put in my place both by the butcher and the queue of housewives, but never once was I treated with anything but good humored tolerance.

The fishmonger was equally kind. Being hard up much of the time I sought fish heads, chicken necks and gizzards[xvi], and bits and pieces that often end up in the refuse bin because for some reason the Europeans were revolted by some of these most nutritious and delicious parts of fish and poultry. "Mr. Jackson," I used to call as I poked my head hopefully round the door. "Can I get a salmon's head?"

He growled, "What — you again?" throwing a damp squelchy parcel in my direction. If he hadn't a fish head he would always find something else; he never sent me away empty handed.

I met with only one rebuff on account of my color during my stay in England. It happened in Derby where I had gone to attend a Trades Council Conference. A room had been booked for me in one of the hotels there but when I checked in, first the receptionist, then the manager, after one look at me, flatly denied that a reservation had been made for me.

The booking, they said as an afterthought, was for 'Stevenson', and it was quite obvious that they resented the fact that a man with a name like Stevens should have a black skin. As I found out later the hotel was not even fully booked at the time.

Although it appeared to be a case of blatant racial discrimination, I did not want to make a fuss about it, but my hosts — the Conference organizers — took strong exception to the attitude of the hotel keeper and went as far as to report the incident to the Secretary of State for Colonies, the Rt. Hon. Arthur Creech Jones, who expressed his regrets. Of course, this was long before the passage of legislation banning racial discrimination in Britain and no legal action could, therefore, have been taken.

Perhaps I was lucky, for, apart from that incident, I found myself readily accepted by almost everyone. Few, except children, even gave me a second glance. "Have you been down a mine, please?" one shy little spokesman of an inquisitive group of youngsters asked me one day.

The family with whom I lodged in Balham when I attended the trade union course at Clapham could not have been nicer and done more to make me feel at home. How loath I used to be to get out of my warm bed and be slapped hard by the sudden impact of the biting cold morning air. If I lingered too long, however, I would hear my landlady's agitated voice calling from the bottom of the stairs: "Shaki, your breakfast is spoiling".

This was as effective as a cannon shot for getting me moving. I was so dumbfounded at the warmth and friendship I found among the Europeans in Britain that it was impossible to connect them with the same breed that were inflicted upon us in Africa. I asked myself time and again: how is it that the Europeans here are so different from the great majority of those who go out to us in the colonies? What changed them so?

How can they ever really know us and understand our feelings when they are so 'far away' from us? Such behavioral change is, of course, typical of an unchecked and unchallenged elite. I remember on one occasion raising this question of elitism when I was at Ruskin, but to my surprise I was not encouraged to pursue it.

"Surely that's hardly a subject of much importance to anyone concerned with trade unions or the labour movement," I was told. Although I accepted this view at the time, I have since become very much concerned with the subject, for in many of the books which I come across dealing with the new African countries I often see references to the elites or new ruling classes which, it is claimed, have emerged in them.

I myself have used the term several times in this book when referring to the privileged few among us who, through opportunities of education or environment, were the first to be given a say in the government of our country.

Elsewhere, however, the references to these elites are generally brief but they seldom fail to leave the impression that an elite group is a dubious thing for an African to belong to. For my part, I am sorry that no African writer I have read has dealt with this subject in any depth, because it is one of very great importance to us. So much so that no matter how inadequate they may be, I feel I must offer some of my own views on it.

I do not wish to speculate about the nature of those who could be described as our own particular elites at this stage, but I can have no reason to think that they are markedly different from those we find elsewhere in Africa, or indeed in the West. The meaning of the term 'elite' seems to be variable so I shall take it here to refer to the few governing the many in all the organizations found in society. Naturally this doctrine raises many questions, such as, how they come into existence, how they maintain themselves in power and above all, how can they be controlled.

The few things I have read about elites have been about those in the West where the subject is receiving more and more attention. Although I did not study it too closely, the book that interested me most on this topic was one entitled *The Managerial Revolution* by an American named James Burnham[xvii], who argues that no matter how much ordinary people try to keep power in their own hands, an elite will grow up from among them, tend to take away that power and largely nullify their ambitions.

Although socialists dedicate themselves to social economic change, the real revolution would come from elite managers in industry and commerce who, by applying their expertise, would take power away from the capitalist owners of the big enterprises and themselves determine their policies.

This would eventually spread to all areas of activity throughout the community and a managerial society would be established. According to Burnham, who, I must point out, was writing during the last war, the same development is taking place in countries which have already established socialism and we must therefore look forward to living in a world completely and consciously dominated by elites of one sort or another

However much one may dislike the way that Burnham develops his argument, his main theme that the few govern the many and should do so, cannot be ignored.

There is no doubt that, whether they have heard of him or not, he has many supporters and it would be foolish to suppose that intelligent and educated Africans are not among them. And this poses a very special problem for us who are in the earlier stages of development.

There can be little doubt that the vast majority of people, both in Africa and throughout the Western world, accept without question the fact that the few govern the many and, moreover, that the governing few like it that way for no other reason than to secure for themselves the enjoyment of privilege, power and wealth.

There is however a sizeable minority who, whilst acknowledging this to be a fact of life, do not necessarily agree with it but feel that no great improvement can be brought about in their own lives unless they accept it, believing that their prosperity comes in the wake of the successful few and that there is no other way of achieving it. This is the minority which exercises so much influence at general elections.

It is noticeable, and natural, that ordinary people only see elitism where it makes its greatest impact upon them, but they do not see its ramifications. They know that the thing exists and they tend to leave it at that unless they feel compelled to fight it because of an attack upon some vital interest. They will certainly not have learnt anything about elitism in any education they may have received, and it is understandable that they develop an attitude of helplessness towards it when it discloses itself to them as they take on the responsibilities of adult life.

The charge of apathy which is so often hurled at them by political activists is not as justified as many of them imagine. The so-called indifference voters does not, in my opinion, always stem from a lack interest in how they are governed. On the contrary, it all too often from the firmly held conviction that whichever party they choose to support, they will still not be freed from the pressures which they believe their rulers and managers bring to bear upon them.

Even when they are nurtured in ignorance and are driven solely by their instincts, the behavior of large numbers of people is seldom as irrational as it appears at first sight. But it is not convenient for elites to recognize this because it is essential for their purposes to project the notion that the motives of most human beings are not often guided by reason, and that without their leadership catastrophe would engulf us all.

> *Having gained general acceptance of this notion they then proceed to create an even more powerful myth, namely, that we are under an obligation to submit ourselves to them on the grounds that what is so clearly of such benefit to our society is morally desirable, and therefore our laws should be based on it.*

It seems to me that any theory of society which is formulated by a minority and which makes that minority the principal beneficiaries of its own proposals is suspect from the outset. It might also be added that generally those who voice this suspicion are soon made to realize that they are to be counted among the greatest enemies of the community. The last thing the 'few' are ready to concede in practice is that there should be open competition among elites.

One of the greatest weaknesses of elitist theory would appear to be the sweeping nature of its basic doctrine. While I agree that the influence of a self-conscious 'few' can only too readily be seen in the affairs of organizations all over the world, it by no means follows that this tendency will necessarily continue at either it's present, or on an increased, scale.

If it were really the case that all the highly intelligent men and women who are to be found in the ranks of the rulers, managers and leaders of the hundreds of institutions — including universities — which go to make up the modern state were engaged exclusively in the acquisition of power, wealth and privilege, then the battle for improving and transforming the shape of any society would be lost before it could be joined. But it is here, I think, that the theory, and its practice, falls down.

Even among this comparatively small group it seems obvious to me that the universal belief that all men are not alike is equally true. It is far from being the case that all intelligent men are devoted only to their own advancement. Furthermore, it is important to remember that the ruling classes are not composed exclusively of the most gifted men. Prominent, if not dominant, among them are those who owe their positions entirely to the accident of birth and favorable laws of inheritance. In noting this I should also like to offer a quite different observation which many think is naive.

It is that my life has been greatly influenced by the fact that the very greatest thinkers and artists do not seem to have troubled themselves overmuch about power and wealth, and while it is true that many of them gained fame during their lifetime, many died without any recognition at all.

Unfortunately, the mere modelling of one's behavior on such great men is not sufficient if one is to deal effectively with elite groups in whatever country they appear. Checks and balances must be applied to those who speak for us and act in our name and the particular manner in which this should be done is for each country to determine for itself, always bearing in mind that those rising from the grassroots to apply the checks on our behalf will constitute a budding elite.

It is often overlooked or suppressed by elitists that the main opponents of their outlook have been men and women who themselves originated from social classes which do not normally take a progressive view of society. It is, however, a fact that in the West the contributions of middle and upper class people to the liberalization of the community have been of the greatest importance, and the less developed the country the more important these contributions have shown themselves to be.

Unfortunately it appears to be the case that, all over the world, ordinary people have not reached a sufficiently high standard of education to be able, unaided, to bring about the social reforms they are most in need of. Even in the most advanced countries working class leaders have not emerged in anything like the numbers that are necessary if they are to succeed in playing their rightful part throughout their communities.

It is true that trade unions have become effective within their chosen sphere, but outside this area the field is on the whole dominated by people of the middle or upper classes. This is not to say that working class people do not desire reform; indeed they do, but they are not skilful in either formulating or promoting it and it is here that progressively minded people from other social groups are most fitted to help them. Self-regarding elite types are not normally found in this kind of work. Thus it can be seen that even outside the field of trade unionism the harshness of those in executive authority is moderated very considerably by the activities of people who are equally competent and, above all, equally coherent. It is here that we in a developing country, such as ours is, are seriously handicapped, mostly for reasons which, in my opinion, are part of the colonial legacy.

I was recently asked by Lord Fenner Brockway what I considered to be the disadvantages left by the old colonial regime. Without hesitation, I replied that the most harmful feature about colonialism is that it induces passivity. Because of the inordinately long period of colonial domination which was imposed on the former Colonies, the initiative for independent and thoughtful action in the handling of our affairs was lacking in our mentality when the time came for us to take control.

We had been brought up to look to the colonial masters for everything and had developed a couldn't-careless attitude to matters affecting our own country. If we discovered somebody making away with government property or idling his time at work, we did not see anything wrong in it because we felt anything was justifiable as long as it was against the direct interests of the Colonial masters.

Thus, at independence we had the formidable task of decolonialising our mentality and our outlook to problems of national interest. In other words, we had to re-educate ourselves in our approach to the problems of our country and of the world at large.

People whose only role is the acceptance of direction lose both interest and initiative, and this applies not only to the great mass of the population; it also has a serious effect on those who, had they been in a free society, would have played, as others elsewhere have done, a full part in the life of the country and sought to improve it. But it was characteristic of colonial government and of the commercial and industrial undertakings which tended to follow its lead that it felt that everything except the most innocuous activities came within its purview.

Because of this our better educated classes became inhibited about putting their hand to anything that could in the vaguest sense be described as potentially political. That is why the majority of our political and trade union leaders did not seek employment with the usual organizations. So it came about that anyone who wished either to reform or to protest became a professional, although the term generally applied to him was agitator.

As I see the position in Sierra Leone, we are now in a situation where although groups of leaders have necessarily and speedily come into existence since the mid-fifties, because of the comparatively short period of time that has elapsed since then, we have not witnessed as yet the emergence of corresponding groups who could act really effectively as 'counter-elites', that is, informed people who have a keenly developed awareness of the public good, who are prepared not only to draw attention to the abuse of power but also to promote more enlarged concepts of general welfare, without seeking advantages for themselves.

I have already offered what I believe to be logical reasons for the apparent absence of this type of citizen in the past, and I am not unmindful of the excellent work being done today by a growing number of individuals to ameliorate the conditions of their fellow countrymen.

Nevertheless, the fact remains that much more organizational work needs to be done if their efforts are to be put to the best use and attention is to be focused upon the most urgent of our social and economic needs. The number of men and women who are now in possession of higher education and professional qualifications has increased very rapidly over the past ten years or so, and I feel that too few of them have expressed their social consciousness in practical terms.

Perhaps much of this reluctance to engage in new areas of endeavor is due not only to induced apathy, but also to the mistaken impression that all social activity should stem from the Government. In view of our history, this attitude is quite understandable; nevertheless, it stands in dire need of correction.

The total good that can flow to a people can never be provided by a government. Ideas for social and economic improvement are not engendered solely by official departments, as those of us who are familiar with the West very well know. In Britain, for instance, not only do non-governmental organizations inspire legislative and other reforms; they also concern themselves with their proper implementation if they are enacted by Parliament.

The idea of specialized groups working within groups is also found in Britain; one that springs to mind, which was well known to many of us, was the Colonial Section of the Fabian Society, itself an off-shoot of the Labour Party. It must now be clear to us that, where we have not already done so, we must begin to envisage a structure in our society in which governing and controlling groups must continue to play an essential and permanent part.

In this respect, we will be no different from other countries. We can, however, unlike most of them, take realistic steps at the outset to consider how far the presence of these groups should lead us to build a society in which they will not dominate, but rather participate, in a community life in which other social groupings will also and integral part. I believe it is very important for us to recognize the need for this fully and openly. It is well worth the trouble to study the conventional views of elite groups in advanced countries. Without exception they first lay down that entry to any of them can be based only on merit and, in the first instance, the criterion is generally intellectual.

Then the would-be candidate must further prove himself by passing the relevant specialist examinations to secure full entry into the group, and the success he obtains at this stage can be of great help to him in the subsequent progress he can make inside. In some cases, this success can be overvalued and sometimes lead to the rapid promotion of men who, although intellectually distinguished, find it difficult to understand the viewpoint of ordinary people.

However, as a general principle we can hardly quarrel with the idea that a man should offer some proof of his intelligence before he is accepted as a member of a ruling group. It only remains to discover whether entry to these groups is open to all so that the community can benefit from all of its members who are capable of directing its affairs. To this the answer is invariably in the affirmative, but closer investigations often reveal that there are pre-conditions for entry which are themselves thought by many to be socially divisive, but since these are not imposed by the groups, their affirmative answer can hardly be challenged. In the light of all this it might well be asked what reasonable objections can be made against the claims of those who consider that they are best fitted to be in control of the most important organizations in the country.

Although it is often put in more elegant language, the short answer to this question is that tests of cleverness bear no relation to moral worth, and in the modern world we are becoming increasingly aware of the fact that governments and commerce and industry are faced with moral issues which are in every way as real as those which are faced by individuals.

While it is true that a man may be both clever and good, we have no reason to believe that there is a necessary link between the two qualities. The main charge against the elitists is that they tend to obscure this fact and to imply that the mere possession of intelligence is of itself indicative of moral responsibility. My reading of history does not confirm this.

The position then, as I see it, is that while it is essential for our wellbeing that we should elect and appoint competent men and women to conduct the affairs of the public organizations in our country, it is fair to neither us nor them to assume that they will always seek the best interests of the community. We must continue to accept the need for checks and balances not merely in the shape of regulations where these appear to be necessary, but also for creating more public awareness of the organizational life of the country. I urge this because no greater stimulus can be found for encouraging those in control of our affairs to give of their best than the continuing development of such activities.

Up to now I have discussed this subject mostly in terms of elites and, as I describe them, 'counter-elites'. There is, however, another very important element to take into account if we are to move ultimately into a fully self-conscious democratic state: the will of the majority of the people. It is hardly surprising that past elites have shown little inclination to take account of them, especially with regard to their potentialities in society.

But it appears to be true of ruling groups everywhere that they find it difficult to convince themselves that ordinary people are ever able to initiate policies which really are for their own good, and they are equally reluctant to concede that their own particular sort of intelligence should be less able to see the essentials of a situation than the collective common sense of those who happen to be most affected by it.

One of the greatest deceptions practiced on the mass of the people is to persuade them that if they have a choice of political parties from which to elect a government, they are living in a *fully* democratic community. This proposition is obviously specious if the leaders of the parties on offer are wedded to the concept of elite government, because they will never agree that every voter should be as influential as they are themselves in the determination of policy, and it is noticeable that their support for democracy tends to wane if the masses do not follow them blindly. What they look for are adherents, not for people who wish to participate in the process of governing.

I believe that the best proof that a party can offer to a people of its true democratic intentions is by heeding the natural similarities between men in society rather than their differences. I have never heard anyone advocate absolutely flat equality of treatment for everyone and for the foreseeable future I do not think I could give my mind to the notion.

Nevertheless, we in our Party believe that every man and woman has a body, a mind and a soul, and each one of them is entitled, as far as we can provide them, to all the means that are necessary for the full development of these endowments.

On the other hand, we shall tolerate no groups who regard themselves as supermen and require that they must be treated as if they were a different species from the rest of us. Only if we can grasp the vital importance of this approach can we hope to combat the dangers of ruling groups which aim to take possession of our people and country.

As I have pointed out, we must have men in positions of power throughout the whole of our society, and vities. If we are sensible we will choose the most competent men from among those who, happily, are available to us. But let us see to it that we do not charge this group with responsibilities which we have no right to ask them to accept. By this I mean that if it is not made clear to our leaders in of the all walks of life that we hold men accountable for their actions, then we can have no justifiable complaint if they adopt policies which do not to their meet with our wishes.

Men who are under effective direction will tend to follow the instructions of those who control them, but if control is not applied to them, then they have no alternative but to devise both their own policies and the manner in which they are carried out.

On the other hand, leaders are seldom unresponsive if those who appointed them maintain a continuing interest in their activities.

We are too easily persuaded that all abuses of power stem from the malpractices of leaders when in fact their true origins arise from the abdication of control by those whom these from leaders represent.

Sometimes it is difficult to draw the line between interfering with the proper administration of an organization and of the expressing legitimate concern about its progress. At our stage of development, we should not be unduly worried if in seeking the latter, we find ourselves unwittingly guilty of the former.

Elitism is something which has always existed everywhere in the world in one form or another, and my observations are intended to make us recognize this fact. It would be extremely foolish of us to imagine that we can escape its dangers more easily than others have done unless we adopt a policy directed to this end. As I have indicated, I believe such a policy can be formulated in a manner flexible enough to serve the varying circumstances in which we will find ourselves in the future. First, of course, must come the frank recognition of the problem itself; along with a refusal to accept the view, too prevalent in the world that no remedy can be found for it.

With this premise must come an acceptance of the need to encourage, and to fully organize, those among our educated people who wish to apply themselves increasingly to those programmes of social and economic welfare which are already part of our development. There is a great and immediate need for this.

Secondly, there is the need to apply ourselves to the realization of our aim for the education of our people, failing which elitism must prevail. There is an assumption behind Abraham Lincoln's famous statement about government *by* the people which is often overlooked. Without knowledge men cannot effectively govern themselves either as individuals or as communities, though knowledge can often be derived from experience and does not necessarily imply a formal education.

During this study period in England, I discovered a great deal about trade unionism which gave me heart. It was only then that I realized that difficulties are inherent in any attempt to establish workers' organizations in any country, whether it is 'developed' or not. I was astonished to learn that during the period of the early British trade union movement, the workers were no more responsive to disciplined membership than I had found my own to be.

In many ways, this was the chief and most encouraging lesson I learnt in England. Before this, I had tended to despair of ever seeing a really closely knit and influential movement in Sierra Leone; but when I discovered that our faults were similar to those which had plagued the early leaders of the British unions, I took fresh heart. Not, I may say, because they too had sometimes been as ineffectual as our own, but because it showed that in conditions of ignorance the reactions of all men are much the same and that Sierra Leonean workers were not uniquely backward.

Looking back now it seems odd that some of the most valuable things I learnt at Oxford were in a sense only incidental to the main purpose of my stay there; which was to get a real understanding of the administration of modern trade unions and to get a good grasp of the British system of industrial relations. In fact, when I left Sierra Leone we already had a system which was quite a creditable version of the British one. As regards trade union administration, it soon became clear to me that our organizations were far too small to be able to gain much benefit from British methods.

Nevertheless, I learnt a great deal at Oxford and also a great deal going about the country. For instance, I was particularly interested to find that the average worker in the United Kingdom was just as indifferent to the affairs of his union as I had found my own people to be. I discovered that it was not uncommon in a branch of perhaps three thousand members for the secretary to have to make special efforts to see that a dozen or so turned up for the monthly branch meeting to provide the necessary quorum.

At first, I was appalled by this as I had been in similar circumstances in Sierra Leone. Later I came to understand what I believe to be the real reason for this seeming indifference; the elite-creating tendency of large numbers of poorly educated men.

In any group, large or small, there are invariably a few members who take a continuing interest in any organization for their mutual benefit. The general membership tend to regard these individuals as their natural leaders since they are better informed and more coherent than themselves and, furthermore, they are workers like themselves. Because of this, I believe they observe an unspoken compact. They feel that their own attendance at meetings is not necessary because they are convinced that if any new benefits can be assured, their natural front- line leaders will be at the meeting doing all that can be done to get it.

So, in their own minds, they are far from indifferent to the real purposes of their union, as is readily shown whenever it is thought expedient for them to show their massed strength. There are obvious dangers in this, but it is difficult to persuade the rank and file that this is so because they are quick to point out that unlike other elites, their leaders seek neither social nor financial gain in the course of their activities on their behalf. This is a powerful argument to rebut notwithstanding those instances where we know that this loyalty has been abused.

EPILOGUE

The title that I chose for this book speaks for itself. It was life and the process of experience that taught me the most important and relevant parts of what I know today.

This is not to deride the usefulness of a conventional education at various levels. We all can and should learn from others willing to impart their knowledge to us, whether in the classroom, the auditorium, the laboratory, orally or through their writings. We should attempt to acquire even a very small fraction of what other men and women have learnt and discovered through the centuries in all fields of knowledge, especially in the ones in which we are interested, and to which we feel we can make our own contribution.

But I strongly feel that much academic knowledge is liable to remain useless unless it is combined with experience - the experience which enables one to assess the relevance of the acquired knowledge, or parts of it, in a given situation, to select what is applicable, to modify it as may be required by circumstances, and then to apply it in the light of one's instinct and judgment, in the light of what life has already taught us.

Like any educational institution, life teaches only those who want to learn from it, and many are those who stubbornly refuse to absorb the lessons it so freely offers, relying exclusively on formally acquired knowledge rather than attempting to combine it with their own experience.

Some of our young men and women returned from abroad with impressive academic qualifications but proved totally incapable of adapting their knowledge to circumstances, of making it relevant in our environment. I am sorry to say that in some cases neither they, nor the country, could benefit from their education. A few have remained convinced that Sierra Leone and its people should change, if only to enable them to apply successfully the theories that they had been taught.

These Sierra Leoneans could be compared to a few of the expatriate experts and advisers whom we have had over the years; experts who firmly believed that their advice would have produced miracles if only our people and our country had been different from what they are. I deliberately said "a few of the experts and advisers" for many have shown a more flexible and pragmatic approach to our problems and a deeper understanding of our people.

Over nearly two and a half decades of independence, for example, we have been advised by well-meaning or interested "experts", both foreign and Sierra Leone an, to spend our meagre resources on projects and sophisticated equipment which, however useful elsewhere, did not always fit our requirements and could not be effectively used by our people.

At the time of writing these pages, we suffer from an imbalance in our foreign trade resulting in a shortage of foreign currency, an ailment which we have in common with many other African and developing countries. A classic remedy which foreign advisers have urged us to apply- a remedy which has undoubtedly proved successful in other circumstances- is to promote exports and penalize imports by drastically devaluing our currency. In our country, it is argued, producers of export commodities, such as gold, diamonds or coffee, receive, in real terms, less than world market prices for their goods - a situation allegedly amounting to a disincentive to increase production.

At the same time, the experts argue, officially imported goods are subsidized in effect by virtue of the prevailing rate of exchange, making it possible for ordinary people to buy essential commodities at prices which, in real terms, are indeed lower than those obtained on the world markets.

According to the knowledge and logic of the foreign experts, reversing the situation, that is making imported goods more expensive in local currency while increasing the gross income of miners and other producers of export goods, would help balance our foreign trade by increasing the volume of our exports and reducing the volume and, therefore, the cost of our imports. If we paid a bonus to our exporters of gold and diamonds (as some other countries do to promote their respective exports) instead of expecting them to sell their goods through official channels for admittedly less than what they could get on the world markets, we might even find that some goods are smuggled into our country to benefit from a higher price here, rather than out of it. Naturally, this is a tempting thought.

I am not an economist, but what life and my knowledge of our people have taught me is that the level of production of most of our export goods will not increase significantly as a result of higher prices. But a significant increase in the prices of basic imported goods, on which much of the population depends for their day-to-day existence, would inevitably result in higher wages to make up for the increases and, consequently, in greater inflation. For, unlike in some other countries, the living standards of most of our people are so low that no downward adjustment could be contemplated or tolerated and any attempt to bring them down would be fraught with the danger of political destabilization.

Moreover, the consumers of imported goods are far more numerous in our country than the producers of export commodities who, incidentally, would also be affected by the higher prices of imported items which they consume, cancelling out the effect of the higher income they would receive for their efforts and making nonsense of the incentives supposed to promote a higher level of production. Nor, of course, would our suppliers in the industrialized world benefit from a reduction in our imports which would only bring them more unemployment.

Unfortunately, it is not only foreign experts who tend to be carried away by figures and what appears to be irrefutable logic, ignoring the complexity of the human factor and delivering their definitive verdict as if the people expected to apply their theories could be programmed like computers.

Some years ago many of our people became incensed by the high and rising prices of imported commodities, including what many regarded as essential items. It was well known, of course, that both the importers and the distributors of these items were making substantial profits at the expense of our consumers, despite the so-called competition among the various businessmen. Moreover, it was also known that our importers, most of them expatriates, could not or would not order goods in sufficient quantities to secure the lowest prices from their suppliers abroad.

In the circumstances, it stood to reason that if a state-owned corporation or organization were to buy the essential goods in bulk, directly from producers or manufacturers abroad, and distribute them directly to the public through its own retail network, on a non-profit basis, by-passing not only the importers but also the wholesalers, retailers, and other middlemen, prices to the end consumer would be appreciably reduced.

The logic of the argument seemed irrefutable and, moreover, the theory was reported to have been borne out in practice in many countries where consumer cooperatives had proved successful. Though I had some intuitive reservations at the back of my mind, I could not but subscribe to what seemed to be so obvious a solution to our problem by supporting the establishment of the National Trading Co., or N.T.C. as it became known,- a state-owned enterprise enjoying the full financial and moral support of our government. In theory, at least, the N.T.C. should have been able to compete so successfully with private enterprise as to drive the "sharks" out of business and eventually achieve a virtual monopoly of trade in specified areas. For once, both socialist and capitalist economic analysis concurred in leading us to expect this outcome.

In practice, however, the result of our venture vindicated neither. It is now obvious that even though the venture may not have been a total failure, it certainly did not justify our confidence and its benefits fell very short of our expectations. Some would still argue that the idea was basically good and would have offered the anticipated benefits if only this or that had not happened, or if some people had not acted as they did. I fully agree with this analysis, but what life has taught me is that what actually happened was not as unpredictable and unlikely to happen as some people would like to think, regardless of the measures we may have taken to prevent it from happening.

We have now accepted the relative failure of the experiment, put it down to experience and written off the financial losses which, in the event, were not unbearable. For if life has not yet taught me how to avoid making any mistakes, it has taught me at least to recognize them and to desist from persisting to advance along an uncharted road which may turn out to be more treacherous than appearances suggest.

In political matters too we have had our share of advisers and well-wishers, some more sincere than others. They too have often failed to realize that not everything that glitters is gold; that social and political doctrines, however attractive in theory, cannot be applied in practice if they do not take into account the reality of the society in which they are intended to operate. *An architect can choose the materials best suited for his design. A politician must choose the design best suited for the material at his disposal - the people he wishes to serve.*

I do not dispute the advantages of some political theories, nor the fact that they may have been successfully applied in this or that country. But life has taught me that one man's meat can be another man's poison- one of the few adages which my own experience has often confirmed. At one end of the scale we have always had those who want us to copy faithfully the western type of democracy; at the other, those who would like us to emulate the Marxist system as it functions in some countries.

Both groups can produce fairly convincing arguments, but neither has bothered to assess the chances of successfully reproducing a working model of the original in our circumstances; and both have conveniently ignored what would happen if we ended up with a broken down parody of the original - a parody resulting in untold dislocation, hardships and bloodshed.

Some of our African leaders, too, appear to have swallowed hook, line and sinker the political and economic theories propounded by foreign doctrinaires, including theories which are known to have failed in other countries, and have attempted to apply them in Africa at their own risk and at the expense of their people.

Some of these leaders are no longer with us but I knew them well. I have not the slightest doubt about their patriotism, their sincerity and their selfless and relentless efforts to do everything in their power to improve the welfare of their respective peoples, to uphold the dignity and sovereignty of their countries and to promote the freedom and unity of Africa. What may be open to some doubt and what has been questioned by some of their own nationals is whether the methods and policies which they adopted in good faith to achieve their lofty aims were workable in practice and appropriate for the purpose.

Whatever the answer to this question may be, the fact is that the situation in many African countries today, especially the economic situation, falls far short of expectations and has been almost unanimously recognized in some cases as very serious. What could have gone wrong? Can drought, world recession and other natural and man-made calamities beyond our control provide the whole answer?

Anthropologists tell us that Africa was the cradle of mankind. It has certainly been inhabited by intelligent human beings for far longer than most other parts of the world. The countries which are now faced with serious food shortages and other enormous difficulties were able to feed themselves for millions of years, long before the human race began to settle in Europe and America. Though still suffering from neo-colonialism, our countries are no longer subjected to the shameful and blatant exploitation experienced during the colonial era. Most of them now benefit from a measure of foreign assistance which was unknown until about 25 years ago.

Could it be that some of the doctrines and theories imparted to us in good or bad faith by non-Africans since the new age of independence may have proved more lethal than the bullets we used to receive in the more distant past? In the exact sciences researchers test a theory in the laboratory and, if the experiment fails, they either try again, using different methods, or conclude that the theory was wrong. All they stand to lose is their time and effort.

In politics, economics and other areas directly affecting the lives of human beings one cannot take such risks; one cannot resuscitate the thousands who may have died or been sacrificed in the process of attempting to make a dream come true; one cannot offer adequate compensation to those who were led to believe that the unattainable could be attained if only a sufficient number would willingly shed their blood on the altar of an untested theory.

Hardly any bank nowadays would risk its money by financing a project before reliable feasibility studies have established its profitability. Would it not be wise for ordinary people to insist on political and economic feasibility studies before agreeing to risk their freedom, their livelihood and even their lives on projects fraught with the danger of ruining their countries and subjecting a whole nation to greater hardships and frustrations than those which a reckless minority had fought to remove. What has often baffled me in history is how many good and sincere people have struggled selflessly for years only to bring about, in objective terms, the very opposite of the lofty ideal which they had set out to attain.

Historians sometimes attribute these tragic failures to "unforeseen developments" or to circumstances beyond the control of those foolhardy leaders who, giving them the benefit of the doubt, attempted to put everything right without envisaging that something could go wrong. A wise and prudent man would know that though the sequels of some political changes cannot be predicted with any degree of accuracy in an area where one deals with imponderable human factors, one could predict with certainty that unpredictable situations may arise. What life has taught me is to aim at the most desirable, hope for the best, but always expect the unexpected and never rule out the worst.

In my own view, however, the tragic failure of some attempts to solve a wide and complex range of problems with a magic wand is often due not so much to the unpredictable as to the inadequate ground work done by those who spend so much time visualizing a bright future that they are left with too little time to study the past and analyze the present. Yet, in social and political edifices, the future can only be built on the foundations of the past and within the framework of the present

Sometimes, I have the feeling that even when they try to analyze the present, some politicians, or would-be politicians, fail to do so objectively, lest a fair assessment should jeopardize their aspirations and explode their theories; or else, they reject anything that does not fit into their subjective analysis. Nor would they always assess objectively the experience of others in similar circumstances, especially if some aspects of that experience tend to contradict their preconceived pattern.

I am not suggesting that the experience of others should always be a determining factor. But totally to ignore the effect of policies which have proved counter-productive in similar situations could be as dangerous as to follow blindly a course of action simply on the ground that it is supposed to have been successful elsewhere.

Life has taught me to make my own judgements in which the experience and example of others carry some weight without ever becoming decisive; it has also taught me to distinguish between wishful thinking and real thinking for practical purposes; to divorce emotions (which we all have) from the sober assessment of reality and, occasionally, to express the former while acting only on the basis of the latter.

In the political field, I have learnt that if people are to participate in the implementation of policies these must relate to their traditions, their natural talents, attitudes and propensities. Conceiving policies which, however desirable, go against the grain of the people, or are out of keeping with their experience, and then rely on persuasion, compulsion or so-called education to change the people so as to make the policies acceptable and applicable, is what I would regard as a recipe for failure; except, perhaps, in the very long run, by which I mean centuries rather than decades.

What life has taught me is to observe and try to understand people, assess their attitudes and aptitudes, their qualities as well as their inherent weaknesses and to accept both as part of reality; to appreciate that some of their basic instincts, good or bad, are too deeply rooted in pre-history to be significantly changed, except in the very short term, by fine rhetoric, coercion, decree, Act of Parliament or even Revolution; in short to see people as they are and not as some would like them to be or imagine them to be. Finally, in the light of what life has taught me, I have learnt to be tolerant and patient and neither to expect too much from people nor to look down upon them or to underestimate their ability and potential.

In practical terms, especially during the latter years of my political career, this has led me to discourage policies and legislation, which, however desirable in theory, might prove

142

counter-productive because their successful implementation or enforcement would depend too much on the competence, dedication and integrity of people who may not always prove up to the envisaged task.

By the same token, life has taught me to favour methods which, though perhaps far from the theoretical ideal in a modern society, are more in keeping with the traditions of our people, their culture and their instinctive approach to the solution of problems. In this context, it has also taught me to distinguish between the desirable and the possible, to make allowances for human nature, to blend firmness with compassion and, above all, perhaps, always to remember that no one is infallible. This leads me always to allow for the possibility of my own judgment being wrong, as well as that of my closest associates.

There was a time when, like most young men, I had an unshakable confidence in my own views. Life has taught me to recognize my mistakes in all humility and to revise my judgment whenever the evidence calls for such a course. In other words, life has taught me that no education is ever complete and that the essential lesson of life is that one must continue learning from it to the end of one's days.

One of the things which I have learnt throughout my life is that, however strong and confident one may feel, there is a limit to how far one can go it alone. We are all prone to face crises in our health, our endeavors, our emotional lives and our careers. Occasionally, we are bound to feel that we may have taken the wrong turn and are walking along the wrong path. Past mistakes make us conscious of the risk of future ones and of the dangers which have claimed so many victims. This is especially so in the case of politicians and leaders who are conscious of the fact that a possible error of judgment on their part would affect not only their own lives but also those of their fellow citizens whose number may run into many millions.

There are situations when one feels that, despite one's confidence and apparent power, one is at the mercy of forces which one can neither understand nor control- forces which reach beyond one's experience. Something which life taught me in my early childhood and has been teaching me ever since is that if one is to avoid the danger of succumbing to these forces, one needs guidance and strength from without- a permanent anchor which can help one keep on an even keel in fair weather and save us from floundering in a raging storm. To me, such an anchor is God, although I accept that some people may give their anchor a different name.

I am convinced that God's help is freely available to all those who genuinely seek it. Rejecting it, I feel, is not a sign of strength, but one of extreme presumption bordering on reckless folly, for history is yet to identify the man or woman who never made a serious mistake and never needed moral and spiritual support from a superior force outside his or her comprehension. But life has also taught me that what most of us can expect from God is strength and guidance rather than miracles.

While life has taught me that no one is infallible, it has also taught me that no one is invariably wrong and that there is often a good deal of truth and merit in what may appear at first sight to be a load of nonsense. This has led me to listen more attentively to what others may have to say, to learn from what life may have taught them and, if possible, to put it to the test.

I am certainly not an opponent of change. In fact I spent much of my life fighting for change and reforms which appeared to many to be radical, or even revolutionary. I fought for the rights of our mineworkers because I knew that their working conditions could be improved as a result of resolute action on our part. I fought for the full sovereignty and independence of our country because I knew that our goal was within our reach and that our aspirations could be fulfilled if we went about in the right way. I fought for a more equitable social order in our country and against its domination by people from any particular region, tribe or social class because I knew that this too could be achieved, providing a healthy foundation for further development.

I remain convinced that there is much room for change and improvement in every sphere, and not only in Sierra Leone. The world has been changing ever since its creation and will undoubtedly continue to change, for better or for worse.

In fact, the world in which we now live differs vastly from the one into which I was born and grew up as a child. Much of what we see today in our homes and in our streets and which we take for granted would have been unimaginable in my own youth. Real hunger, as we experienced it at times, is now virtually unknown in our country. Though housing is still a problem no one need die of exposure to the elements or walk barefoot. Clothing is no longer the major problem that it was.

Infant mortality and death from curable diseases has been greatly reduced. Education has become available to the great majority and certainly to those who really want it. Electricity and piped water, both still unknown in my early childhood, are enjoyed by a constantly growing number, including virtually all those who live in our major towns and cities.

How many of those who so frequently and vehemently complain about the efficiency of our public transport, the shortage of government cars or the cost of petrol are conscious of the fact that their grandfathers, or even their fathers, had to walk barefoot along miles of forest paths and risk their lives in rickety canoes to cross rivers now spanned by concrete bridges.

In the more distant past people lived in a fairly static civilization and died in an environment almost identical to the one in which they were born. They did not realize that change was possible and, therefore, did not clamor for it. The extent of the changes which I have witnessed in my lifetime exceeds by far anything that happened in the previous 500 or even 1000 years. Nowadays the craving for change seems to have become addictive and the faster the rate at which some people witness it, the more they want to speed it up.

What life has taught me is the importance of trying to distinguish between what can be changed rapidly with a good chance of success, what is subject to slow change or evolution, and what should be left alone because it is not ripe for change or because it is so rigid and brittle that any attempt to change the status quo would involve too great a risk of disintegration and a waste of effort, resources and human lives.

Moreover, even a change that appears to be both possible and desirable can never be guaranteed to be successful. This, I believe, applies not only in politics and economics but also in other spheres. I have seen machines which had to be written off as a result of attempts to improve their performance, servicable houses which collapsed in the course of modernization, farmers and businessmen who ruined themselves in the process of expanding their operations or making them more profitable, and people who died or were crippled after surgery intended to cure them.

Unfortunately, I think, these considerations are often ignored by those who, having taken a quick look at our situation and the structure of our society, immediately decide that everything is fundamentally wrong and should be changed forthwith. I very much hope that life will eventually teach them its realities as it has taught them to me - realities which are not always pleasant or easy to accept. I have now learnt to accept them with serenity rather than resignation and this is perhaps the most important lesson which life has taught me a lesson which guides not only my approach to politics and to my personal affairs, but also my attitude to life itself and to its inevitable end.

For this lesson I also owe a debt of gratitude to the American poet William Cullen Bryant[xviii] (1794 - 1878) whose *Thanatopsis* made a profound impression on me in my youth, though it was only in more recent years that I began to appreciate the full significance of his words:

> *So live, that when thy summons comes to join*
> *The innumerable caravan, which moves*

To that mysterious realm, where each shall take
His chamber in the silent halls of death,
Thou go not, like the quarry-slave at night
Scourged to his dungeon, but, sustained and soothed
By an unfaltering trust, approach they grave
Like one who wraps the drapery of his couch
About him, and lies down to pleasant dreams.

Pictures

MY FATHER- ALIMANY JAMES STEVENS- IN THE LATE 1920S

PICTURE TAKEN AT THE END OF 1960

ON THE CAMPAIGN TRAIL

FAMILY PICTURE TAKEN IN 1982

WITH MY GRANDSON, SIAKA "BORIS" STEVENS AND HIS MOTHER, YVETTE

MY WIFE, LADY REBECCA STEVENS

With two of my many Grandchildren, Francis & Alex

WITH ONE OF MY DAUGHTERS, FRANCESS AND DR. S.S. MAGONA

MY SON JENGO, MY SON-IN-LAW AUGUSTINE AND DR. PAT ON
THEIR FIRST DAY IN PARLIAMENT 1982

MY WIFE AND ONE OF MY DAUGHTERS, THELMA

THREE OF MY CHILDREN, JONGOPIE, THELMA AND ALEX, WITH
MY SON IN LAW, IB TEJAN JALLOH AND MY NIECE JOSEFINE

PERFORMING OFFICIAL DUTIES

PERFORMING OFFICIAL DUTIES

PERFORMING OFFICIAL DUTIES

COMMONWEALTH MEETING

SEKOU TOURE, PRESIDENT OF GUINEA

WITH GENERAL YAKUBU GOWAN

WITH JIMMY CARTER IN 1979

PERFORMING OFFICIAL DUTIES

Index

U

W

Y

Endnotes

[i] In political economy and international relations, conditionality is the use of conditions attached to the provision of benefits such as a loan, debt relief or bilateral aid. These conditions are typically imposed by international financial institutions or regional organizations and are intended to improve economic conditions within the recipient country. The International Monetary Fund (IMF) in the early 1980s imposed harsh conditionalities for loans to African countries. These conditionalities would include, devaluation of the local currency, removal of subsidies on essential goods and drastic reductions in public expenditure. For many African countries that heavily depended on imports of essential items (rice and fuel), the devaluation of their currency meant increase in prices of imports and since subsidies were not allowed, the consumer had to bear the full price rise.

[ii] **Moyamba** is the capital and largest city of Moyamba District, in the Southern Province of Sierra Leone, with a population of 11,485 in the 2004 census. The population of the city is ethnically diverse, although the Mende people make up the majority. The city is home to the Hatford Secondary School for girls, which is one of the elite secondary schools in Sierra Leone. The school attract some of the most gifted students from all parts of Sierra Leone and abroad. The school is an all-girls secondary school, and the students are in a boarding home in the school campus. The city has a history of producing some of Sierra Leone's most prominent politicians, including the country's first president Siaka Stevens.

Like the rest of the country, football is the most popular sport in Moyamba. The biggest and most popular club from the city is the Yambatui Stars, which currently plays in Sierra Leone second division.

[iii] I have lived in Norway for the past 24 years, a country that is known for its economic success and according to the United Nations Human Development Index, the best country in the world to live in.

Remarkably, this is a country where the notion of community,that we are all in it together, that the wealth of the coutry belongs to all and that we help and take care of each other is what dominates in politics.

[iv] Dr Fred M Hayward is a specialist on higher education with more than 25 years of experience as an educator, scholar, and senior administrator. He has taught at the University of Ghana, Fourah Bay College and the University of Wisconsin-Madison, where he was professor of political science, department chair and dean of international programmes. Dr Hayward has written extensively on development issues and higher education.

[v] Siaka Stevens has 15 children and over 70 grandchildren. While most of his children still live in Sierra Leone, the majority of his grandchildren resides in Europe, Asia, The Americas, Africa and Australia.

[vi] The **Limba** people are a major ethnic group in the Republic of Sierra Leone. They form the third largest ethnic group in the country, about 8.5% of Sierra Leone's total population (about 566,529 members). The Limba are Indigenous people of Sierra Leone and speak various dialects of a language largely unrelated to other tribal languages in Sierra Leone. They are primarily found in the Northern Province, particularly in Bombali District, Koinadugu and Kambia District. During Sierra Leone's colonial era thousands of Limbas migrated to the capital city of Freetown and its Western Area. As a result, a significant number of Limbas can be found in Freetown and its surrounding Western Area. During the 16th, 17th, and 18th century, many Limba people were shipped to North America as slaves.

The Limba are mainly rice farmers, traders and hunters who live in the savannah-woodland region in the Northern Province of Sierra Leone. They predominate in 7 of Sierra Leone's 149 rural chiefdoms, and their community affairs are dominated by the local paramount chiefs.
They also have a past and current interest in politics, for

example Siaka Stevens as the first president of Sierra Leone from 1971-1985, Christian Alusine Karamara-Taylor as a founding member of the All People's Congress and Paolo Conteh, the current defence minister. **Source: Wikipedia.**

[vii] The **Vai language**, alternately called Vy or Gallinas, is a Mande language, spoken by roughly 104,000 in Liberia and by smaller populations, some 15,500, in Sierra Leone. Vai is noteworthy for being one of the few sub-Saharan African languages to have a writing system that is not based on the Latin script. The **Vai syllabary** is a syllabic writing system devised for the Vai language by Momolu Duwalu Bukele of Jondu, in what is now Grand Cape Mount County,Liberia. Bukele is regarded within the Vai community, as well as by most scholars, as the syllabary's inventor and chief promoter when it was first documented in the 1830s. It is one of the two most successful indigenous scripts in West Africa. Vai is a syllabic script written from left to right that represents CV syllables; a final nasal is written with the same glyph as the Vai syllabic nasal. Originally, there were separate glyphs for syllables ending in a nasal, such as *don,* with a long vowel, such as *soo,* with a diphthong, such as *bai,* as well as *bili* and *sɛli.* However, these have been dropped from the modern script.

The syllabary did not distinguish all the syllables of the Vai language until the 1960s when University of Liberia added distinctions by modifying certain glyphs with dots or extra strokes to cover all CV syllables in use. There are relatively few glyphs for nasal vowels because only a few occur with each consonant.

One of Momolu Duwalu Bukele's cousins, Kaali Bala Ndole Wano, wrote a long manuscript around 1845 called the *Book of Ndole* or *Book of Rora* under the pen name Rora. This roughly fifty page manuscript contains several now obsolete symbols. The Vai syllabary was added to the Unicode Standard in April, 2008 with the release of version 5.1.

Source: Wikepedia

[viii] The **Distinguished Service Order (DSO)** is a military decoration of the United Kingdom, and formerly of other parts of the Commonwealth of Nations and British Empire, awarded for meritorious or distinguished service by officers of the armed forces during wartime, typically in actual combat.

Instituted on 6 September 1886 by Queen Victoria in a Royal Warrant published in the *London Gazette* on 9 November, the first DSOs awarded were dated 25 November 1886. It is typically awarded to officers ranked major (or its equivalent) or higher, but the honour has sometimes been awarded to especially valorous junior officers. During the First World War, 8,981 DSOs were awarded, each award being announced in the *London Gazette*.

The order was established for rewarding individual instances of meritorious or distinguished service in war. It was a military order, until recently for officers only, and normally given for service under fire or under conditions equivalent to service in actual combat with the enemy, although it was awarded between 1914 and 1916 under circumstances which could not be regarded as under fire (often to staff officers, which caused resentment among front-line officers). After 1 January 1917, commanders in the field were instructed to recommend this award only for those serving under fire. Prior to 1943, the order could be given only to someone mentioned in despatches. The order is generally given to officers in command, above the rank of captain. A number of more junior officers were awarded the DSO, and this was often regarded as an acknowledgement that the officer had only just missed out on the award of the Victoria Cross. In 1942, the award of the DSO was extended to officers of the Merchant Navy who had performed acts of gallantry while under enemy attack.

[ix] **Isaac Theophilus Akunna Wallace-Johnson** (1894 – 10 May 1965) was a **Sierra Leonean** and **British West African** workers' leader, journalist, activist and politician. Wallace-Johnson was born to poor **Creole** parents in **Wilberforce Sierra Leone**, a village adjoining the capital city, **Freetown**. His father was a farmer, while his mother [79]

was a fishwife who sold her goods in markets in neighboring villages. Many of his relatives held low-status jobs involving craftsmanship, carpentry and masonry. His poor upbringing and low social status influenced his understanding and empathy of the working class, as seen in his early association with communism and later, his leadership in the West African labor movement, he emerged as a natural leader in school. After attending United Methodist Collegiate School for two years, he dropped out and took a job as an officer in the customs department in 1913. He was dismissed for helping organize a labor strike, but later reinstated to his position a year later. After resigning from his job, he enlisted as a clerk with the Carrier Corps during World War I. After being demobilized in 1920, Wallace-Johnson moved from job to job, before settling as a clerk in the Freetown municipal government. He claimed to have exposed a corruption scandal, which resulted in the incarceration of top officials, including the mayor. After being fired from this job in 1926, he left Sierra Leone and became a sailor. He joined a national seamen union and it is believed that he also joined the Communist Party. In 1930, he helped form the first trade union in Nigeria and attended the International Trade Union Conference of Negro Workers in Hamburg, where he established a number of contacts. He published articles and edited the *Negro Worker*, a journal devoted to uniting black workers around the world. He traveled to Moscow, where he claimed to have attended classes on Marxism-Leninism theory, union organization and political agitation.

x The **Mende people** are one of the two largest ethnic groups in Sierra Leone, their neighbours the Temne people having roughly the same population. The Mende and Temne both account for slightly more than 30% of the total population. The Mende are predominantly found in the Southern Province and the Eastern Province, while the Temne are found primarily in the Northern Province and the Western Area, including the capital city of Freetown. Some of the major cities with significant Mende populations include Bo, Kenema, Kailahun and Moyamba.

The Mende belong to a larger group of **Mande** peoples who live throughout West Africa. The Mende are mostly farmers and hunters. The Mende are divided into two groups: The *halemo* are members of the *hale* or secret societies, and *kpowa* are people who have never been initiated into the hale. The Mende believe that all humanistic and scientific power is passed down through the secret societies.

The Mende speak the **Mende language** among themselves, but their language is also spoken as a regional lingua franca by members of smaller Sierra Leonean ethnic groups that inhabit the same part of the country. Their language is spoken by around 46% of Sierra Leone's population. Source: Wiki

[xi] The **Sierra Leone Creole people** (or **Krio people**) are an ethnic group in Sierra Leone. They are the descendants of freed African American, West Indian and Liberated African slaves who settled in the Western Area of Sierra Leone between 1787 and about 1885. The colony was established by the British, supported by abolitionists, as a place for freedmen. The settlers called their new settlement Freetown Today, the Krio comprise about 4% of the population of Sierra Leone.

Like their Americo-Liberian neighbors in Liberia, Krio have varying degrees of European ancestry because some of the settlers were descended from White Americans and other Europeans. Alongside the Americo-Liberians, the Krios are the only recognised ethnic group of African-American, Liberated African, and West Indian descent in West Africa. As with their Americo Liberian neighbors, Creole culture is primarily westernized. The Krios developed close relationships with the British colonial power; they became educated in British institutions and held prominent leadership positions in Sierra Leone under British colonialism.

The vast majority of Creoles reside in Freetown and its surrounding Western Area region of Sierra Leone. The only Sierra Leonean ethnic group whose culture is similar (in terms of its integration of Western culture) are the Sherbro. From their mix of peoples, the Creole developed what is now the native Krio language (a mixture of English and indigenous West African languages). It has been widely used for trade and communication among ethnic groups and is the most widely spoken language in Sierra Leone.

The Krios are primarily Christians at just over 80%; while a significant minority are Muslim. The Krio Muslims are widely known as **Oku** and are the descendants of intermarriage between the freed slaves and Muslim Liberated Africans, who were mostly Yoruba from Southwest Nigeria who settled in Freetown in the mid 19th century.

Due to their history, the vast majority of Creoles have English surnames. Many have both English first names and last names. Most of the Krio Muslims have Islamic first names, though the vast majority of them have English surnames as well. Due to their history as descendants of historically Yoruba communities, many Creoles have Yoruba middle names. Source: Wiki

[xii] The term **Cockney** has had several distinct geographical, social, and linguistic associations. Originally a pejorative applied to all city-dwellers, it was eventually restricted to Londoners and particularly to the "Bow-bell Cockneys": those born within earshot of Bow Bells, the bells of St Mary-le-Bow in east London's Cheapside district. More recently, it is variously used to refer to those in London's East End, or to all working-class Londoners generally.

Linguistically, Cockney English refers to the accent or dialect of English traditionally spoken by working-class Londoners.

[xiii] A **lighterman** is a worker who operates a lighter, a type of flat-bottomed barge, which may be powered or unpowered. In the latter case it is today usually moved by a powered tug.

[xiv] **Hematite**, also spelled as **haematite**, is the mineral form of iron(III) oxide (Fe_2O_3), one of several iron oxides. Hematite crystallizes in the rhombohedral lattice system, and it has the same crystalstructure as ilmenite and corundum. Hematite and

ilmenite form a complete solid solution at temperatures above 950 °C (1,740 °F).

Hematite is a mineral, colored black to steel or silver-gray, brown to reddish brown, or red. It is mined as the main ore of iron. Varieties include *kidney ore*, *martite* (pseudomorphs after magnetite), *iron rose* and *specularite* (specular hematite). While the forms of hematite vary, they all have a rust-red streak. Hematite is harder than pure iron, but much more brittle. Maghemite is a hematite- and magnetite-related oxide mineral.

[xv] **Haidara Kontorfilli** (born 1890-1931) was a Sierra Leonean charismatic Islamic religious reformer and an anti-colonialist from the Mandingo ethnic group who championed the cause of the rural masses in Kambia in the Northern Province of Sierra Leone.

His surname derives from a Mandingo word which could be freely translated as meaning an enigma, or a thorn in the flesh. It is possible that this was not Haidara's original surname, and represented popular recognition of the challenge he posed to the colonial government.

Haidara Kontorfilli was born in 1890 in Kambia, a town located in the Northern Province of Sierra Leone to Mandingo parents from French Guinea (now Guinea). At his hometown of Kambia he healed the sick, and from where he disseminated his religious teachings. His influence spread quickly and widely, and he attracted a considerable followers. He stressed the need for religious reform, directing his teachings mainly to the poorer people, and acting as the guardian of their interests. In a letter to he wrote to Kambia District Commissioner, he warned the people of Kambia to change their ways and convert to Islam or face death.

At this juncture, the colonial administration became alarmed and confused, seeing his teachings and pronouncements as a threat to the stability of the government. On February 9, 1931, the British colonial administration served Haidara with an expulsion order, charging him with sedition. Haidara ignored the order and, in reply, wrote an open letter to the people of Kambia which among other things told them not to fear the British, and to refrain from paying the hated house tax, a proposal which made plenty of sense to the peasant masses hard pressed by the raging economic depression at the time. In effect, the letter was an open challenge to the very foundation of the colonial regime, and amounted to a declaration of war against it. The reaction of the colonial administration was to despatch troops of the Royal West African Frontier Force stationed in Kambia to effect Haidara's arrest at Bubuya.

Haidara, determined not to submit to the humiliation of an arrest, proceeded to organise and arm his followers with machetes, swords and guns in readiness for the inevitable encounter. The confrontation which took place on February 16, 1931 was brief. Haidara succeeded in killing the commanding British officer but he and four of his men were killed almost instantly, and the other protesters were dispersed.

Haidara Kontorfilli was clearly a heroic and charismatic leader, courageous and invested with considerable organisational abilities. His commitment to his own ideas and beliefs as well as to the interest of his followers was unquestionable, and in the end he sacrificed his life for both. Source: wiki

[xvi] The **gizzard**, also referred to as the **ventriculus, gastric mill**, and **gigerium**, is an organ found in the digestive tract of some animals, including, some fish and some crustaceans. This specialized stomach constructed of thick, muscular walls is used for grinding up food, often aided by particles of stone or grit. Source: Wiki

[xvii] **James Burnham** (November 22, 1905 – July 28, 1987) was an American philosopher and political theorist. A radical activist in the 1930s and an important factional leader of the American Trotskyist movement, in later years Burnham left Marxism and turned to the political Right, serving as a public intellectual of the American conservative movement, and producing the work for which he is best known, *The Managerial Revolution*, published in 1941.

[xviii] William Cullen Bryant (November 3, 1794 – June 12, 1878) was an American romantic poet, journalist, and long-time editor of the *New York Evening Post*. The title comes from the Greek *thanatos* ("death") and *opsis* ("sight"); it has often been translated as "Meditation upon Death". Bryant wrote the bulk of the poem in 1811 at age 17, and it was first published in 1817 by the *North American Review*. He added the introductory and concluding lines 10 years later in 1821.

Made in the USA
Columbia, SC
23 February 2022

56668798R00102